CHRIST THE CENTER

Larry D. Baskin
3.13.80

HARPER'S MINISTERS PAPERBACK LIBRARY

CHRIST THE CENTER

Dietrich Bonhoeffer

A new translation by
Edwin H. Robertson

Published in San Francisco by

HARPER & ROW, PUBLISHERS

New York, Hagerstown, San Francisco, London

This translation was published in England under the title CHRISTOLOGY.

First Harper & Row paperback edition, newly translated, published in 1978.

The text of this book is printed on 100% recycled paper.

Library of Congress Cataloging in Publication Data

Bonhoeffer, Dietrich, 1906-1945.
  Christ the center.

  (Harper's ministers paperback library)
  Translation of Wer is und wer war Jesus Christus?
  Includes bibliographical references and index.
  1. Jesus Christ—Person and offices—Addresses, essays, lectures. I. Title.
BT201.B4713   1978   232   78-4747
ISBN 0-06-060811-7

  79 80 81 82 10 9 8 7 6 5 4 3 2

CONTENTS

PART THREE
THE ETERNAL CHRIST

(No manuscript has been preserved)

TRANSLATOR'S PREFACE

The popular conception of Bonhoeffer is of a theologian who would have done away with all the religious elements of the Church and perhaps even with the Church itself. As a radical theologian, he is not thought of as one who gets to the root of the matter, as the word implies, but as an iconoclast. There are certainly many sentences in his *Letters and Papers from Prison* which, when quoted out of context, give credence to this view. Yet he was and remained a Lutheran and a very orthodox churchman. His last act before he died was to conduct a religious service, and there are many points in the closing letters that indicate his unwillingness to be too destructive. To quote but one: 23 August 1944, 'I am often shocked at the things I am saying, especially in the first part [i.e. of his theological work and with special reference to a chapter on 'Taking Stock of Religion'], which is mainly critical. I shall be glad when I get to the more positive part. But the whole subject has never been properly thrashed out, so it sounds very undigested. However, it can't be printed at present and will doubtless improve with waiting.'[1]

The more positive side, which was never written down, can only be recovered by study of his earlier writings, and it is for this reason that the publishers have tried to give the English-speaking public as much Bonhoeffer in English as possible. Quite clearly, not everything that Bonhoeffer wrote was good, but almost all he wrote helps us to reconstruct the positive side of his thinking at a time when only the negative appears to be known. Of course, there must be selection, and this small book, which contains reconstructed lectures given by Bon-

[1] *Letters and Papers from Prison*, SCM Press (London) and Macmillan (New York), 1971, p. 393

hoeffer in 1933 on the theme of christology, needs justifying. There are two obstacles to be overcome.

First, this is not Bonhoeffer's text – it has been reconstructed from notes by his students. With so much genuine Bonhoeffer material still not translated, why pick on this doubtful text? The answer is that christology is at the heart of Bonhoeffer's theology and that Eberhard Bethge is better qualified than any man living to reconstruct what Bonhoeffer really said. Here we can listen to Bonhoeffer, not talking about Bonhoeffer's contribution to christology, but Bonhoeffer lecturing on christology and making his contribution as he goes along. There is much in these lectures that we should expect to find in any lectures on christology, but through an examination of this material we come very close to the mind of Bonhoeffer. The question he is answering is not, 'What do you think of Christ?', a question he would have rejected; but, 'How has Christ been understood and what is wrong with the classical concepts of christology?' There are many reasons why we need to understand 'Bonhoeffer's christology' if we are to understand what he intended to write in a positive way about the Church in his chapter on 'Taking Stock of Religion'.

A second objection is that this series of lectures was given in 1933. This is an early date, before most of the great events in Bonhoeffer's life had taken place, and before he had matured his thought about the Church. Our scientific way of thinking has accustomed us to discount what is old and read only the new. This is unwise in philosophy or theology. Certainly, the later writings are a development of the earlier and have taken into account the impact of later events and the fruit of much further thought. But a theologian will often assume what he has already written and leave his later writings to add to his earlier rather than replace them. There is clear evidence that Bonhoeffer is such a theologian. In a letter he wrote after the failure of the July plot in 1944, he questions his famous book, *The Cost of Discipleship*, with words that are significant: 'I thought I could acquire faith by trying to live a holy life, or something like it. It was in this phase that I wrote *The Cost of Discipleship*. Today I can see the dangers of this book, though,' he adds, 'I am prepared to stand by what I wrote.'[1] Later, as he explains in that letter, he learnt that only by living in this world completely could he acquire faith. What he had written in 1937 might have to be modified, but not cancelled. He still sees holiness as a way to faith, but now it is 'worldly holiness'.

Bonhoeffer's attitude to christology in 1933 was not annulled by later thought or experience. It remained the basis of his thinking about Christ. If today we are to understand what he meant by the Church it is essential to read these lectures. Even then, they are incomplete, for Bonhoeffer never finished the course. Like some of Leonardo da Vinci's works, they tell us much and make us long for more. At least we have as much as his students had. Martin E. Marty, in his introduction to the chapter on the lectures in *The Place of Bonhoeffer*,[2] writes of them: 'In the four-volume Collected Works, no single piece can compete for interest and importance with Bethge's recomposition of these lectures from students' notes'; and the author of the chapter itself, Jaroslav Pelikan, says, 'This is one of the most positive essays in the book.' I would strongly recommend that admirable chapter[3] as a commentary on Bonhoeffer's christology. It alone would be enough to justify the translation of these lectures into English, and their publication as a major event in the presentation of the thinking of Bonhoeffer to the English-speaking world. Neither the date, nor the unfinished state of the text, should keep us from giving very careful attention to what they contain.

Having disposed of the two possible objections, it might be

---

[1] *Letters and Papers from Prison*, p. 369
[2] SCM Press (London) and Association Press (New York), 1963, p. 143
[3] *The Place of Bonhoeffer*, pp. 145-64

well to look at the positive reasons for putting this text into English. Some have already been indicated. The main reason is the importance of the subject – at any period in his life, christology is the key to Bonhoeffer's thought. This is evident in the way he deals with his most radical problems. At the Berlin Youth Conference in April 1932, the young Bonhoeffer denounced the appeal to 'orders of creation' in a discussion of war and peace. He saw the danger of declaring that anything was good because it was made good. The appeal to Genesis 1, with which he had just been wrestling in the lectures that later became *Creation and Fall,* seemed to him specious and dangerous. When God declared creation 'very good', he spoke of an unspoiled creation and not the world we know. For 'orders of creation' he substituted 'orders of preservation'. In writing up this discussion in a report for *Die Eiche,* Bonhoeffer explained the difference: 'The difference was that in the light of the concept of orders of creation, ordinances and features of the world were regarded as valuable, original, "very good" in themselves, whereas the concept of orders of preservation meant that each feature was only a feature preserved by God, in grace and anger, in view of the revelation of Christ. Any order under the preservation of God was set and directed by Christ and only preserved for his sake. An order is only to be regarded as an order of preservation so long as it is still open for the proclamation of the Gospel. Where an order is basically closed to this proclamation, be it apparently the most original – marriage, nation, etc. – it must be surrendered. The solution of general ethical problems . . . must be sought only in the revelation of God in Christ, and not from orders of creation.'[1]

Already in 1930, in his inaugural lecture which had as its theme, 'Man in Contemporary Philosophy and Theology',

[1] *No Rusty Swords,* Collins (London) and Harper & Row (New York), 1965, p. 180

he summarized his survey of the treatment of 'man' in terms of christology. The key passage has been quoted by Dr Pelikan in his own translation.[1] I would prefer to use my own translation, from *No Rusty Swords*, not because of any basic disagreement but because I prefer the solution John Bowden and I found to the insoluble problem of the translation of *'Gemeinde'* to the equally valid translation used by Dr Pelikan. Whatever *Gemeinde* does mean in this context, both of us have recognized that it does not mean 'congregation'. I hope Dr Pelikan will forgive me for using 'Church' more sparingly than he does, and at times translating it with the preferred Bonhoeffer concept of 'community'. In retranslating these lectures now I have found myself coming nearer to Dr Pelikan in his translation of *Gemeinde*. The passage is as follows: 'It is the mystery of the community that Christ is in her and, only through her, reaches to men. Christ exists among us as community, as Church in the hiddenness of history. The Church is the hidden Christ among us. Now therefore man is never alone, but he exists only through the community which brings him Christ, which incorporates him in itself, takes him into its life. Man in Christ is man in community; where he exists is community. But because at the same time as individual he is fully a member of the community, therefore here alone is the continuity of his existence preserved in Christ. Therefore man can no longer understand himself from himself, but only from Christ.'[2]

It was a straight line of development from this early inaugural lecture to the draft of his major work on Ethics, still unfinished at the end.[3] In that, he rejected the 'formation' that sought to impose morality from without, but built his new

[1]*The Place of Bonhoeffer*, p. 146
[2]*No Rusty Swords*, p. 68
[3]*Ethics*, SCM Press (London) and Macmillan (New York), 1955

morality upon a renewal of the mind from within as in Romans 12:1-2. This process of renewal, with no outward forces trying to impose an alien pattern on the mind but rather an inherent growth shaping the mind until man becomes what he is, was seen as the growth of the mind to be like that of Christ. This was more than the 'imitation of Christ'; it meant the power of Christ working within until man becomes fully human – Christlike, because that is what man is intended to be. All else is less than human. And so humanity again depends for its authenticity on Christ.

Before turning to the lectures themselves and the events of the year in which they were given, I should like to consider a letter which Bonhoeffer wrote to his friend on 8 June 1944.[1] Eberhard Bethge had obviously asked a series of theological questions which were troubling him and apparently also Bonhoeffer. The answer he gets is not the crystal clear reply of a theologian, but the puzzling response of an honest and not yet clear believer. The only thing Bonhoeffer feels absolutely sure of is his attitude to Christ. Of the questions, he says, 'I should be happy if I could answer them all myself,' and goes on, in a passage which shows his real genius and the reason why his letters continue to be read by men who still seek answers to the fundamental questions: 'I am led on more by an instinctive feeling for the questions which are bound to crop up rather than by any conclusions I have reached already.' There follows a brilliant analysis of the failure of contemporary theologians to realize the full seriousness of the questions raised. In a historical preamble he traces the impact of the Renaissance – giving the thirteenth century as his estimated date when this movement towards the autonomy of man had reached a measure of completeness. Since then, he claims, 'Man has learnt to cope with all questions of importance without recourse to God as a working hypothesis.' And so,

[1] *Letters and Papers from Prison*, pp. 324-9

'what we call "God" is being more and more edged out of life'. The world becomes sure of itself and the Church gets more and more frightened. Then it makes the mistake of trying to bring in God and Christ to counter this trend. That makes the movement towards autonomy anti-Christian. The fatal mistake of the Church was to try to 'prove to a world come of age that it cannot live without the tutelage of "God"'. The inability to maintain this in the face of the world's autonomy leads to the 'ultimate questions', where God now takes refuge. Here at least he is needed.

At this point comes Bonhoeffer's most quoted question, a rhetorical one: 'But what if one day they [i.e. these ultimate questions] no longer exist as such, if they too can be answered without "God"?' Bonhoeffer shrewdly points out that secular equivalents to religion play the same game. These are the existentialist philosophers and the psychiatrists who 'demonstrate to secure, contented, happy mankind that he is really unhappy and desperate and merely unwilling to realize that he is in severe straits he knows nothing at all about, from which they alone can rescue him'. This is held up to ridicule, in order to attack even more vehemently the Christian apologetics that take the same line. The attack on the adulthood of the world is defined as 'pointless, ignoble and un-Christian'. This failure is ascribed by Bonhoeffer to a misunderstanding of Christ. The central question for him concerns the relation of Christ to the newly matured world. Liberal theology failed because it allowed the world to assign Christ his place in the world. Bonhoeffer was a true disciple of Harnack in his appreciation of the strength of liberal theology. Yet he saw that it failed – 'in the dispute between Christ and the world it eventually accepted the comparatively clement peace dictated by the world'. But at least liberal theology saw that the battle had to be fought, even if it were lost to the superior forces of the world. This acceptance of the battle led to its overthrow. The Church reacted with a return to the Bible and the Reformers. Bonhoeffer shows the inadequacy of many of his contemporaries in their attempts to deal with the world come of age. Heim tried to convince modern man that he is faced with an alternative – despair or Jesus. Althaus reiterated Lutheranism and tried to gain a place in the world for Lutheran teaching and Lutheran worship. Tillich attempted to interpret the evolution of the world in a religious sense: 'the world unseated him and went on by itself: he too sought to understand the world better than it understood itself, but it felt entirely *mis*understood and rejected the imputation.' All these, says Bonhoeffer, were 'sailing in the channel of liberal theology'. Barth first realized this and called in the God of Jesus Christ against religion – the spirit against the flesh. This Bonhoeffer believes to be the greatest of Barth's contributions. He finds it in the second edition of his *Commentary on the Romans*. In his *Dogmatics*, Barth showed the Church how to make the distinction between 'religion' and Christ. But he too failed to enable the Church to discover a non-religious interpretation for its theological concepts. This was his limitation. This failure mattered a great deal to Bonhoeffer because Barth passed it on to the Confessing Church which, in its resistance to the German Christians and also to Nazism, lapsed into a conservative restoration of the orthodoxy of the Reformation. Bultmann of course did see Barth's limitation, as clearly as Bonhoeffer did. But he too comes under fire for misconstruing the problem in terms of liberal theology and hence going 'off into the typical liberal reduction process'. Commenting on Bultmann's demythologizing, Bonhoeffer says, 'I am of the view that the full content, including the mythological concepts, must be maintained. The New Testament is not a mythological garbing of the universal truth; this mythology (resurrection and so on) is the thing itself – but the concepts must be interpreted in such a way as not to make religion a pre-condition of faith. Not until that is achieved will liberal theology be overcome and the question it raises be genuinely taken up and answered.' He adds a little later, 'The world's coming of age ... is better understood than it understands itself, namely on the basis of the Gospel and in the light of Christ.' He does not answer his question whether this leaves room for the Church or whether religion is gone for good. But even in his most radical statements about 'religion-less Christianity', he is most careful to preserve a clear christology. It is the structures of religion that must go, not the proper consideration of Christ.

In these lectures on christology, Bonhoeffer is not prepared to find a category for Christ. His questions are not, 'How is it possible for Christ to be both man and God?' His question about Christ is never, 'How?', but always, 'Who?' He will not even have a disguised 'What?' or 'How?' in the form of a 'Who?' Every avenue of his thinking leads him to confront Christ and ask, 'Who art thou, Lord?' or to be confronted by Christ and hear his question, 'Whom do you say that I am?'

The material translated in this book is the substance of a series of lectures given during the summer semester (May-July) in 1933 at the University of Berlin. The original manuscript has not survived and the only text we have is what Eberhard Bethge could reconstruct from the notes of his fellow students. More than once, in his letters, Bonhoeffer shows his complete confidence in Bethge to interpret his thinking. When he was not able to complete his *Ethics* he took consolation from the thought that he had talked it all out with Bethge and that he would fill in the blanks. He has done so admirably here. But the last section is missing because Bonhoeffer never finished the course. This section cannot be written up and that is a pity because he tells us that it was to have dealt with 'The Eternal Christ'. It could have been an important addition to our understanding of Bonhoeffer's thought.

The lectures thus reconstructed, with all their limitations, give us a glimpse into the mind of Dietrich Bonhoeffer as he dealt with his most important theme in the year 1933. The year is significant. Earlier that year, Adolf Hitler had been elected Chancellor of Germany, the Church had had its first taste of a National Bishop, and the issue between the Confessing Church and the German Christians had been defined. Most men knew that a struggle was about to begin which would be for the soul of Germany. None saw this more clearly than Bonhoeffer, who entered the struggle with reluctance. That summer, on the day of the church election, which was to put the German Christians into power and give Hitler the means whereby he could control the Church, Bonhoeffer preached a sermon telling of his reluctant decision to enter the struggle. His text was the classical text for the understanding of the nature of the Church, Matthew 16:13-18. After announcing his text, he declared his reluctance: 'If it were left to us, we would rather avoid the decisions which are now forced upon us; if it were left to us, we would rather not allow ourselves to be caught up in this church struggle; if it were left to us, we would rather not have to insist upon the rightness of our cause and we would so willingly avoid the terrible danger of exalting ourselves over others . . . And yet, thank God, it is not left to us.'[1] That church election and the sermon took place at the end of the summer semester in which Bonhoeffer had given his lectures on christology. The events, in which he was so deeply involved, may explain why the series was never finished. This kind of interference with his academic work also explains why he was reluctant to enter the struggle. Bonhoeffer knew that his theology was important and he also knew that involvement in political struggle, even church political struggle, would distract him from his work. It is important to recognize that Bonhoeffer regarded himself principally as a theologian. This tension was with him when

[1] *No Rusty Swords*, p. 213

he delivered the lectures contained in this book.

During the previous year, his main concern had been with his two major interests – Christian Ethics, or 'Ethics' as he preferred to call it, and the Church. Both themes required a clarification of his christology. He had already made it quite clear that he accepted no authority for the Church except that of Christ 'living and present in it'. At a Youth Peace Conference that year in Czechoslovakia, he had made this clear: 'From Christ alone must we know what we should do. But not from him as the preaching prophet of the Sermon on the Mount, but from him as the one who gives us life and forgiveness, as the one who has fulfilled the commandments of God in our place, as the one who brings and promises the new world . . . Thus we are completely directed towards Christ.'[1] This talk to the Youth Conference and the paper written a little earlier on 'What is the Church?' were both influenced by lectures he gave in 1932 on 'The Nature of the Church'. These lectures compelled him to face the Ecumenical Movement with the need for a theological basis. That was why the talk in Czechoslovakia from which I have just quoted is called, 'A Theological Basis for the World Alliance'. All this intellectual activity was demanding a clear christology and the lectures in this book were prepared as much for Bonhoeffer's own use as for that of his students.

One further influence before we turn to the lectures themselves. In the autumn of 1932, Bonhoeffer worked over his lectures on the early chapters of Genesis, which were later published as *Creation and Fall*. The lectures add very little to the understanding of Genesis 1-3, which they set out to expound, but they nevertheless caused a stir among the students. They posed for Bonhoeffer and his students the question of the place of Christ in creation and the relation of the work of Christ to the fall of man in the setting of a fallen

[1] *No Rusty Swords*, p. 166

17

world. Having raised this problem, he was committed to a series of lectures on christology. The Genesis lectures had already shown the influence of events on Bonhoeffer's thinking. Events themselves were now demanding a clear statement on christology. The church struggle in Germany would require a theological basis as much as the World Alliance did, and that would later depend very much upon Bonhoeffer. The statement when it came was called the Barmen Declaration, and, although Karl Barth was the main theological influence behind the Declaration, it could not have been written without the earnest thought that Bonhoeffer was now giving to christology.

This is one of the things that gives importance to these lectures. They stand between the developing theologian, influenced by all that he had read and thought on the great doctrinal issues, and the leader of the resistance, who was determined that this resistance would be theological rather than political. Here, in this christological material, is an arsenal from which the Confessing Church would draw many of its weapons to defeat the German Christians and thus prevent the poison of Nazism from destroying the Church. That is why the material has a polemical note.

And now to the lectures themselves. They were divided into three parts, of which only the first two were delivered. The first part dealt with the Christ ever present in the Word, the Sacrament and the Church; the second part dealt with the Christ of history. One day a bold theologian will write the third part, on the Eternal Christ. Perhaps this is a task for Eberhard Bethge now that the Biography is finished.

Bonhoeffer refused to begin his lectures on christology with what he called the 'alchemy of the incarnation'. Much discussion of the two natures seemed to him impertinent and certainly concerned with the wrong questions. The discussion which set out to ask, 'What?' had been led into asking, 'How?' and that was no question for man to ask. Equally, he saw how the evasion of christology in the preaching of the cross led to a concentration upon the works of Christ to the exclusion of the real questions. The theologian must be able to speak of Jesus Christ as one in whom 'Act' and 'Being' are one. He is not required to answer the question 'How?', but is required to look seriously at the questions 'What?' and 'Where?' These Bonhoeffer proceeds to deal with.

'What is Jesus Christ?' leads to three answers – 'Word', 'Sacrament' and 'Church'. The development of this can be read in the lectures. The strongest part of it is his discussion of the meaning of the Word. But those who have formed an opinion of Bonhoeffer's thought from his last letters, particularly on the Church, should pay careful attention to his 'high' doctrine of the Church and the sacrament.

'Where is Jesus Christ?' leads to an examination of the self. Bonhoeffer turns to the Reformers for his understanding of Christ as 'for me'. The locus of Christ is therefore found 'standing in my stead' and at the border of my existence. It is because I am separate from my true being that Christ thus stands between me as I am and me as I should be. He stands to judge and thereby to 'rediscover the authentic centre of my true being'. This is not the idealist's attempt to describe Christ as the centre of my being, which really means that the human personality is the highest expression of man and his point of contact with God. One does not therefore reason from human experience to Christ, but the other way. Christ interprets our being. We discover our humanity in him. He judges us from the border of our existence and he brings us new life. This argument can be traced carefully in these lectures and it remained important in Bonhoeffer's thinking. Without this, he could not have written his *Ethics*, and only by understanding this insight can we properly follow the argument in his last letters. Here, and especially in the first part, we have the basis for an understanding of such phrases as 'the man for others', 'man come of age'. These lectures are also necessary if we are to correct the false impression of Bonhoeffer as the apostle of the 'dying Church' or as the advocate of 'religionless Christianity' or 'worldly holiness'. The paradox of the catch-phrases can only be resolved by the study of his christology. Only thus can Bonhoeffer guide the post-war Church as he knew he would.

When Bonhoeffer made his fateful decision in July 1939 to return to Germany, he wrote to Reinhold Niebuhr, 'I will have no right to participate in the reconstruction of Christian life in Germany after the war if I do not share the trials of this time with my people.'[1] One of the assumptions he made was that he would be needed after the war in Germany. He was right. But had he remained in America we might have had his help in the rebuilding of the Church and the spiritual life in Germany and Europe after the war. He would certainly have completed his lectures on christology. By returning, he did more. He was able to remain in touch with the different pressures up to the time of his death, and he comes to us through his writings, not as a pre-war theologian but as one who lived it through. His last writings are sealed with his blood and are his legacy to a post-war Europe. The effect they are now having on our theological development indicates how right his decision was.

Our principal danger today is that we shall only use those writings that came out of the experience of his last days. This would be an injustice to one of the greatest theologians of our time. The lectures in this book are necessary as a basis for understanding what Bonhoeffer was hinting at in the occasional papers from prison. We need both the early framework of his thinking and the brilliant insights that he himself attempts to interpret within this framework. The two together give us the voice of the prophet.

[1] *The Way to Freedom*, Collins (London) and Harper & Row (New York), 1966, p. 246

Bonhoeffer gave three answers to the question, 'Where is Jesus Christ today?' These three answers must be studied in the light of all he said later, because he never abandoned them.

1. Jesus Christ is at the border of *my* existence. With that word 'my' he ended the cold discussion of the nature of Christ as an academic exercise. The question has an answer *for me*, not for the textbook. At the border of my existence, he gives meaning to my existence and he gives the only meaning that makes sense and offers hope.

2. Jesus Christ is the centre and meaning of history. With this answer he rescued his theology from a purely personal experience. His christology is biblical and as such rooted in history. This is more than the true historicity of the man Jesus. This is not just 'the Jesus of history'. Again, Christ is not interpreted from history any more than he is interpreted from my experience. History is interpreted from him, as I am interpreted from him. This alone gives meaning to history and hope. At this point, Bonhoeffer is nearest to Teilhard de Chardin.

3. Jesus Christ is the heart of nature. Bonhoeffer does not deduce from nature that God is at work. He denies that it is possible to deduce God from nature. But he claims that Christ, who is already known, can be recognized in nature. He alone gives meaning to nature and hope. Here, Bonhoeffer is closest to Paul.

These three answers force us away from the classical statement of christology. The Chalcedonian Definition is cold, statue cold, and requires the warm breath of life before it can be recognized as anything to do with Jesus Christ. Bonhoeffer would have us discover the ever-present Christ in our existence, in the purpose of history and in the meaning of creation. Or rather all three are discovered to be meaningful in him.

Since these lectures first appeared in English, the long-awaited biography by Eberhard Bethge has been published. In it Bethge, who reconstructed these lectures from student notes, says that Bonhoeffer felt this series of lectures 'the hardest task he had yet undertaken . . . because he was faced with the task of bringing together, preserving and testing out all he had previously thought, said and attempted'.

Bethge also gives us a description of the scene when Bonhoeffer arose to give the lectures:

'Otto Dudzus reports that during that restless summer an audience of nearly two hundred sat through those demanding lectures:

He looked like a student himself when he mounted the platform. But then what he had to say so gripped us all that we were no longer there to listen to this very young man, but we were there because of what he had to say – even though it was dreadfully early in the morning.'[1]

A note on the translation

When these lectures first appeared in English in 1966, Bonhoeffer was less known to the English reader. Not only had the biography still to appear, but only a small part of the *Collected Works* had been translated. Moreover, we were still strongly under the influence of *Honest to God*, which had put undue emphasis upon certain parts of the *Letters and Papers from Prison*. In that situation, John Bowden gave us an admirable translation. It was readable, persuasive and allowed the reader to discover Bonhoeffer as a theologian. In the ten years that have passed, *Christology*, or *Christ the Center* as it is called in the USA, has played its part and in many colleges has become a textbook. The present translation owes much to John

[1] *Dietrich Bonhoeffer – A Biography* by Eberhard Bethge, Collins (London) and Harper & Row (New York), 1970; issued in paperback by Fount (London) and Harper & Row (New York), 1977, p. 164

Bowden's earlier attempt, because it was done when we were working together on the *Collected Works*. There has now been a demand to prepare a translation nearer to the original in style, making use of all we now know about Bonhoeffer's use of technical words and in a form which is more suited for the study of Bonhoeffer's theology in colleges. This I have here attempted. His use of Latin and Greek, for example, has been retained with translation in brackets; *Gemeinde* has more often been translated 'Church' and as far as possible the tension of his style has been reproduced.

E.H.R.

CHRIST THE CENTER

INTRODUCTION

I. The Unfolding of the Christological Question

Teaching about Christ begins in silence. 'Be still, for that is the absolute', writes Kierkegaard. That has nothing to do with the silence of the mystics, who in their dumbness chatter away secretly in their soul by themselves. The silence of the Church is silence before the Word. In so far as the Church proclaims the Word, it falls down silently in truth before the inexpressible: 'In silence I worship the unutterable' (Cyril of Alexandria). The spoken Word is the inexpressible; this unutterable is the Word. 'It must become spoken, it is the great battle cry' (Luther). Although it is cried out by the Church in the world, it remains the inexpressible. To speak of Christ means to keep silent; to keep silent about Christ means to speak. When the Church speaks rightly out of a proper silence, then Christ is proclaimed.

What we wish to concern ourselves with here is the study of this proclamation. The object of our study can only be shown to us again in the proclamation itself. Here to speak of Christ will be thus to speak in the silent places of the Church. In the humble silence of the worshipping congregation we concern ourselves with christology. To pray is to be silent and at the same time to cry out, before God and in the presence of his Word. It is for the study of Christ, that is, God's Word, that we have gathered together as a congregation. Yet, we are not in church, we are in a lecture hall. We have to work within an academic discipline.

Christology as the study of Christ is a peculiar discipline because it is concerned with Christ who is himself the Word or Logos, from which we also derive the term for study. So that christology is really Logo-logy, the study of study, the

Christ the Center

word of the Word of God. Thus christology is self-evidently *the* science, because it is concerned with the Logos. Were this Logos our own logos then christology would be a matter of the logos reflecting upon itself. But it is the Logos of God. His transcendence makes christology the science *par excellence* because it comes from outside study itself. His transcendence is guaranteed because he is a person. The Logos with whom we are here concerned is a person. This man is the transcendent one.

From this we deduce two things:

1. The Logos is not an idea. Where the idea is thought of as the final reality of the Logos, there can ultimately be no understanding for the central character of, and the pre-eminent place given to, christology.

2. With its claim to be *the* discipline *par excellence* and centre of its own space, christology remains unique. It has no proof by which it can demonstrate transcendence of its subject. Its statement that this transcendence, namely the Logos, is a human person, is presupposition and not subject to proof. The transcendence which we make the subject of proof instead of letting it be the presupposition of our thought, is no more than the immanence of reason which comes to grips with itself. Only a discipline which understands itself in the sphere of the Church is able to grasp the fact that christology is the centre of all disciplines. It is the unknown and hidden centre of the university of learning.

All scientific questions can be reduced to two: What is the cause of X? and, What is the meaning of X? The first question embraces the realm of the exact sciences and the second that of the study of the arts; both belong together. The object X is comprehended by the exact sciences when its causal relationship to other objects is understood. The object X will be comprehended by the appropriate arts discipline when its significance in relation to other known objects is understood. Both are concerned with the question of classification. An

28

unknown object can become known when it is possible to place it in an already existing classification. How does the object X fit into the existing order? The question is directed towards the possibilities of the object, its 'How?' The object is determined, encompassed and recognized by its 'How?', i.e. the immanent, human logos determines the 'How?' of the object by its classification. This becomes important for the question of christology. How can this object be classified?

The ultimate presupposition of man is given to him in his human, classifying logos. What happens when doubt is thrown upon this presupposition of his scientific activity? What if somewhere the claim is raised that this human logos is superseded, condemned, dead? What happens if a counter-logos appears which denies the classification? Another logos which destroys the first? What if the old order of the first logos be proclaimed as broken up, superseded and in its place a new world has already begun? When the human logos is addressed like that, what answer can it give?

First, the human logos repeats its old question: How is such a claim possible? How can it be contained within its structure? It continues to ask about the 'How?' But under this threat to its dominion from outside it now surpasses itself. It forestalls the claim by negating itself and at the same time asserts that this negation is a necessary unfolding of its own nature. This is the ultimate deceit and the final strength of this logos. It is what Hegel has done in his philosophy. This reaction of the logos to the attack of the counter-logos is not a mean defence of the other logos – such as we find in the Enlightenment – it is an important insight into the power of its own self-negation. But self-negation is also a way of self-affirmation. In so far as the logos limits itself it also establishes itself with power. Nevertheless, the logos recognizes the claim of the counter-logos. In this way the attempt to attack its ultimate presupposition appears to have misfired. The logos has assimilated the counter-logos into itself.

But what happens if the counter-logos makes its claim in a totally different form? If it is not only an idea, but 'Word' which challenges the dominion of the logos? If this 'Word' appears somewhere and somehow in history as 'Person'? If he declares himself as judgement upon the human logos and says of himself: 'I am the way, the truth, the life', 'I am the death of the human logos, I am the life of the Logos of God', 'Man with his logos must die; he falls into my hands; I am the first and the last.' What then?

When the Counter-Logos appears in history, no longer as an idea, but as 'Word' become flesh, there is no longer any possibility of assimilating him into the existing order of the human logos. The only real question which now remains is: 'Who are you? Speak for yourself!' The question, 'Who are you?', is the question of dethroned and distraught reason; but it is also the question of faith: 'Who are you? Are you God himself?' This is the question with which christology is concerned. Christ is the Counter-Logos. Classification is no longer a possibility, because the existence of this Logos spells the end of the human logos. Only the question, 'Who are you?', will do. The phenomenon is opened up only by this. He answers only to the question, 'Who?'

The question, 'Who?', is the question about transcendence. The question, 'How?', is the question about immanence. It is because the one questioned is the Son that the immanent question is not adequate. Not, 'How are you possible?', that is the godless question, the serpent's question, but, 'Who are you?' The question, 'Who?', expresses the strangeness and the otherness of the one encountered and at the same time it is shown to be the question concerning the very existence of the questioner. He is asking about the being which is strange to his being, about the boundaries of his own existence. Transcendence places his own being in question. With the answer that his logos has reached its boundary he faces the boundary of his own existence. So the question of transcendence is the question of existence, and the question of existence is the question of transcendence. In theological terms: it is only from God that man knows who he is.

The question, 'Who are you?', is common in daily life. But it is often loosely phrased to amount to the same as the question of classification, the question, 'How?' Tell me how you are, tell me how you think, and I will tell you who you are. This is a secularized reduction of the true question, 'Who?', which is basically the religious question posed for every life. The question, 'Who?', is simply *the* religious question. It is the question about the other person and his claim, about the other being, about the other authority. It is the question of love for one's neighbour. Questions of transcendence and of existence become questions concerning the person. This means that man cannot himself answer the question, 'Who?' Existence cannot emerge out of itself, it remains related to itself and only mirrors itself in itself. Fettered in its own authority it still goes on asking the question, 'How?' The human heart is *cor curvum in se* (the heart turned in upon itself), as Luther says. When we ask, 'Who are you?', then we speak the language of the obedient Adam, but we think the language of the fallen Adam, which is, '*How* are you?' In this way the first language was ruined.

Can we in fact put the austere question, 'Who?', at all? Even when we are asking, 'Who?', can we mean anything more than, 'How?' We cannot. The secret of the 'Who?' remains hidden. The ultimate question of critical thought lies in the dilemma of having to ask, 'Who?', but not being able to.

This means that the question must already have been answered before it could be stated correctly. The question, 'Who?', can only be put legitimately when the person questioned has revealed himself and has eliminated the immanent logos. The question, 'Who?', presupposes an answer which has already been given.

This takes us further: the christological question can only be posed scientifically in the setting of the Church. It can only be put where the basic presupposition, that Christ claims to be the Logos of God, is accepted: there, where men ask about God because they know who he is. There is no general blind seeking after God. Here a man can only seek what has already been found. 'You would not seek me had you not already found me' (Pascal). The same thought is found in Augustine. With this, we have the place where our christological work must stake its claim. In the Church, where Christ has revealed himself as the Word of God, the human logos puts the question: 'Who are you, Jesus Christ, Word of God, Logos of God?' The answer is given, the Church receives it new every day. The human logos seeks to understand it, to ponder it and to explore it.

Two questions therefore must remain for ever excluded from christological thought:

1. The question of whether the answer already given and the Church's corresponding question, 'Who?', can be justified or not. This question has no basis, because the human logos can have no authority to doubt the truth of the other Logos. The testimony of Jesus to himself stands by itself, self-authenticating. That is the backbone of every theology. The 'truth' of the revelation of God in Christ cannot be scientifically established or disputed.

2. The question of how the 'truth' of the revelation can be conceived. This question would mean going behind Christ's claim and finding an independent reason for it. In that way the human logos would be claiming to be the beginning and the father of Jesus Christ. With such an inordinate claim, the human logos strives for a trinitarian form.

With the exclusion of these two questions, there remain the questions of 'Who?', of the being, the essence and the nature of Christ. That means that the christological question is fundamentally an ontological question. Its aim is to work out the ontological structure of the 'Who?', without plunging on the Scylla of the 'How?' or the Charybdis of the question of the 'truth' of the revelation. The early Church foundered on the former; modern theology since the Enlightenment and Schleiermacher, on the latter. The New Testament, Paul and Luther sailed through the middle.

Let us get back to where we started: to what extent is the christological question the central question of scholarship? It is because only in christology is the question of transcendence put in the form of the question of existence. It is because the ontological question is put as the question of the being of a person, the person Jesus Christ. It is by the transcendence of the person of Christ that the old logos is judged and learns to understand its own new and relative status, with its necessary limitation. As *logo-logy*, christology alone makes scholarship possible. But this is to touch only upon the formal side.

The matter of content is more important. Human reason has reached its limits with the question, 'Who?' What happens when the Counter-Logos raises his claim? Man seeks to deny the one with whom he is confronted. Pilate asks, 'Who are you?', and Jesus is silent. Man cannot wait for the answer, because it is too dangerous. The logos cannot endure the Counter-Logos. It knows that one of them must die and it therefore kills the one whom it asks. Because the human logos will not die, the Logos of God, who would be the death of it, must die so that it might live on with its unanswered question of existence and transcendence. The incarnate Logos of God must be crucified by man's logos. The one who compelled the dangerous question must be killed and with him the question.

But what happens if this Counter-Word, which was killed, rises alive and victorious as the final Word of God? If he sets himself up against his murderers? If the crucified one shows himself as the risen one? Then the question, 'Who are you?', is sharpened to an extreme point. Then it remains a living question for ever, over, around and in man, as also does the answer. Man may struggle against the incarnate one; against the risen one, he is powerless. Now he is himself the one who is condemned and put to death. The question is turned round and directed at the human logos, 'Who are you that you ask this question? Are you in the truth that you can ask this question? Who are you then that you can only ask about me, when I restore you, justify you and give you grace?'

The christological question is finally validly formulated only where this responding question has been heard. That man on his side can be asked in this way shows who it is who asks. Only God can ask like that. No man can question another man like that. The only question with which man can now respond is, 'Who are you?' The questions of whether it is true or how it is possible, have fallen away.

In practical terms, what does that mean? The unknown one meets men still today on the road, so that they can still ask only, 'Who are you?', however often they try to avoid it. They must come face to face with him. We may also have to come face to face with Goethe or Socrates. That is part of our culture and our ethos. But far more depends upon our confronting Christ – life or death, salvation or damnation. This cannot be known outside, but in the Church it is seen that all rests upon the sentence, 'And there is salvation in no one else' (Acts 4:12). The encounter with Jesus is fundamentally different from that with Goethe or Socrates. One cannot avoid encounter with the person of Jesus because he is alive. With some care Goethe can be avoided, because he is dead. A thousandfold are the ways that men have used to resist or evade an encounter with Jesus.

For the proletariat, it is easy to depict Christ as allied with the Church of the bourgeois society. Then the worker sees no reason any more to give Jesus a qualified place or status. The Church is one with the stupefied and oppressive capitalist system. But at this very point the working class may distinguish between Jesus and his Church; he is not the guilty party. Jesus, yes; Church, no! Jesus can then become the idealist, the socialist. What does it mean when the proletarian says, in his world of distrust, 'Jesus was a good man'? It means that nobody needs to mistrust him. The proletarian does not say, 'Jesus is God'. But when he says, 'Jesus is a good man', he is saying more than the bourgeois says when he repeats, 'Jesus is God'. God is for him something belonging to the Church. But, Jesus can be present on the factory floor as the socialist; at a political meeting, as an idealist; in the worker's world, as a good man. He fights in their ranks against the enemy, Capitalism. Who are you? Are you brother and master? Are they evading the question? Or are they in their own way putting it seriously?

Dostoievsky let the figure of Christ appear in Russian literature as the idiot. He does not separate himself, but clumsily causes offence everywhere. He does not go around with the great ones, but with children. He is laughed at and loved. He is the fool and he is the wise man. He bears everything and he forgives everything. He is revolutionary and yet he conforms. He does not want to – but he does – call attention to himself just by his existence. Who are you? Idiot or Christ?

One thinks of Gerhard Hauptmann's novel *Der Narr in Christo Emanuel Quint*. Or of the presentation of Christ and the misrepresentation in the writings of Wilhelm Gross and Georg Grosz, behind which lurks the question, 'Who are you really?' Christ goes through the ages, questioned anew, misunderstood anew, and again and again put to death.

It is the same temptation for the theologian who tries to encounter Christ and yet to avoid that encounter. Theologians betray him and simulate concern. Christ is still betrayed by the kiss. Wishing to be done with him means always to fall down with the mockers and say, 'Greetings, Master!' There are only two ways possible of encountering Jesus: man must die or he must put Jesus to death.

The question, 'Who are you?', remains ambiguous. It can be the question of one who knows already that he has been encountered in his very questioning and who hears the responding question, 'Who then are you?' But it can also be the question which when asked means, 'How will I deal with you?' And that is a disguised form of the old question, 'How?' The question, 'Who?', can be put to Jesus only when the responding question has already been heard. Then it is not man who has dealt with Jesus, but Jesus who has dealt with man. Thus the question, 'Who?', which already contains in it the responding question and answer can only be spoken in faith.

So long as the christological question is the question of the human logos, it remains imprisoned in the ambiguity of the question, 'How?' But when it is given voice in the act of faith, there is a real possibility of posing the question, 'Who?'

In building up authorities there are two opposing types: the authority of the office and the authority of the person. When you address a question to one who has the authority of office, you ask, 'What are you?' That 'What?' refers to the office. When you address a question to one who has the authority of the person, you ask, 'Whence have you this authority?' The answer is, 'From you, who recognize my authority over you'. Both questions lead us back to the question, 'How?', and are so classified. Basically, everyone is like me. We presuppose that the person asked is identical in being with me. Those who are recognized as authorities are only bearers of an authority belonging to the community, bearers of an office, bearers of a Word. They are not the office itself, nor the Word itself. Even the prophets are only what they are as bearers of a Word. But what happens when one appears who claims that he is not only a bearer, that he not only has an authority, but that he is that authority; not only that he has an office, but that he is that office; not only that he has a Word, but that he is that Word? Then our being is invaded by a new being. Then the highest authority so far in the world, that of the prophet, is at an end. Such is not only a saint, a reformer, a prophet, but he is the

Son. Then the question is no longer, 'What or whence are you?' Then the question is about the revelation itself.

II. The Person and Work of Christ

Christology is not soteriology. How are the two related to each other? How is the doctrine of the Person of Christ related to that of the Work of Christ? The classical statement is in Melancthon's *Loci*: *Hoc est Christum cognoscere, beneficia eius cognoscere; non quod isti* [i.e. the Scholastics] *docent; eius naturas modos incarnationis contueri* (Latin: to know Christ is to know his benefits, not as the scholastics think, to study the kind of natures in which he is incarnate). If we accept that, the christological question would be referred back to the soteriological one and answered there. Who Christ is would then be known only from his work. It follows that a specific christology would be superfluous. This was an epoch-making point of view and was followed through by Schleiermacher and Ritschl.

Put systematically, the question would be, 'Does the work interpret the person or the person the work?' Luther was fond of saying that it all depends upon whether the person was good: if the person is good then the work also is good, even though it does not always appear to be so. On the other hand, one cannot conclude that because the work is good, therefore the person must be good. The work may appear to be good, but it can still be the work of the devil. The devil appears in the form of an angel of light. The work may appear to be evil, but it can still be God's work. A contrary view would lead directly to a doctrine of justification by works. For Luther, the person interprets the work.

The person cannot, however, be known by us, only by God. 'The Lord knows his own' (II Timothy 2:19). There is then no access to the work, except through the person; and access to the person is barred to us by the mystery of God's predestination. The attempt to understand the person from the work is doomed to failure because of the ambiguity of the work. There is no access to man unless he reveals himself of his own accord. In fact, this happens in the Church in the forgiveness of sins. Here, a man presents himself to his brother as a sinner, confesses and receives forgiveness from his brother. In this way, in the Church, the person of another is known.

The situation in christology can thus be understood by analogy with this experience in the Church. Only if I know who does the work can I have access to the work of Christ. Here everything depends upon knowing the person in order to recognize the work. If he was an idealistic founder of a religion, I can be elevated by his work and stimulated to follow his example. But my sin is not forgiven, God remains angry and I am still in the power of death. Then the work of Jesus drives me to despair about myself, because I cannot follow his example. But if Jesus is the Christ, the Word of God, then I am not primarily called to do the things that he does; I am met in his work as one who cannot possibly do the work he does. It is through his work that I recognize the gracious God. My sin is forgiven, I am no longer in death, but in life. All this depends upon the person of Christ, whether *his* work perishes in the world of death or abides in a new world of life. But how can the person of Christ be comprehended other than by his work, i.e. otherwise than through history? This objection contains a most profound error. For even Christ's work is not unequivocal. It remains open to various interpretations. His work can also be interpreted to show that he is a hero, and his cross can be interpreted as the consummate act of a brave man, true to his convictions. There is no point in the life of Jesus of which one could say with unambiguous conviction that here we see the Son of God, proved to be such by one of his works. He does his work rather in the incognito of history, in the flesh. The incognito of the Incarnation makes it doubly impossible to recognize the Person by his Works:

1. Jesus is man and the argument back from works to person is ambiguous.
2. Jesus is God and the argument back from history to God is impossible.

If this way of understanding is closed there remains just one more chance to gain access to Jesus Christ. This is the attempt to be in the place where the Person reveals himself in his own being, without any compulsion. That is the place of prayer to Christ. Only by the Word freely revealing himself is the Person of Christ available and with that also his work.

Thus the priority in theology of the christological question over the soteriological has been established. When I know *who* he is, who does this, I will know *what* it is he does. However, it would be wrong to conclude from this that the Person and the Work can be separated. We are concerned here with the epistemological connection between Person and Work, as we know it, not as it is in reality. The separation of the question of christology from that of soteriology is necessary only to establish a theological method. For the christological question, by its very nature, must be addressed to the one complete Christ. This complete Christ is the historical Jesus, who can never in any way be separated from his work. He is asked and he answers as the one, who is his own work. But christology is primarily concerned with who he is rather than what he does. To put that into an academic formula: the subject of christology is the personal structure of being of the complete, historical Jesus Christ.

PART ONE

THE PRESENT CHRIST – THE PRO ME

Jesus is the Christ present as the Crucified and as the risen one. That is the first christological statement. His presence can be understood in space and time, here and now. It belongs to the definition of the person. Both come together in the concept of the Church.

Christ, as person, is present in the Church. That is the second christological definition. Only because Christ is present can we question him. This presence is the necessary presupposition for the unfolding of the christological question. Only when preaching and sacrament take place in the Church can Christ be questioned. The understanding of the Presence opens up the way for the understanding of the Person.

This understanding is open to two serious misunderstandings:

a) The presence of Christ can be understood as the influence that emanates from him, reaching into the Church. This is not the presence of Christ himself, but the effect of his historical influence. Christ is here thought of in dynamic terms. His energy is not dissipated in a series of historical events, but progresses undiminished through history. The presence of Christ is thus accounted for in the category of cause and effect.

b) Attempts are made to pass beyond the limits of the historical to make the image of Christ visible. These images are painted again and again, whether by the Enlightenment or the Rationalists – each with his different picture of the inner life of Jesus, as with Wilhelm Herrmann.

Very often both these misunderstandings occur together, as with Schleiermacher. Ritschl may be taken as representing the first, his pupil Herrmann, the second. Both have in common an error in christology. If Christ is understood from his

43

historical influence, he is essentially power, *dynamis*, but not a person. The *dynamis* can be thought of in different ways. It can be the echo of his historical influence or the newly-emerging image of an ideal of the man Jesus. In this the historical force corresponds more with the temporal, the *nunc*; the ideal power, more with the spatial, the *hic*. The former is thought of in the category of cause, the latter in the category of effect.

Christ is then thought of basically, not as Person, but as non-personal power. That is still true when one talks of the 'personality of Jesus'. In this context, 'personality' is the opposite of what is meant here by Person. Personality is the fullness and harmony of those values that were brought together in the phenomenon of Jesus Christ. Personality is basically a non-personal concept. It disappears among the neutral concepts of power and value. And in this way the christological question is lost. Person is beyond the concepts of influence and image, power and value. When one asks about personality, it is 'How?' and 'What?'; but about a person, it is 'Who?' Jesus as personality, power, value is fully explained by his work, and his person by what he does. Then the only possible way is to infer the person from the work.

What is concealed behind this idea of the presence of Christ is the decision not to consider the resurrection, but to stop with the Jesus of the cross, with the historical Jesus. This is the dead Jesus Christ who can be thought of like Socrates and Goethe. Only the risen one makes possible the presence of the living person and gives the necessary presupposition for christology, which is no longer lost in historical energy or the appearance of an ideal Christ.

Luther tried to interpret the presence of Christ from the Ascension. Christ can be our contemporary because he sits at the right hand of God. 'When he was on earth, he was far from us. Now that he is far, he is near to us.' That means that only the risen one, who has ascended to heaven, can be present with us, not one who is only within history. Ritschl and Herrmann put the resurrection to one side; Schleiermacher symbolizes it; in so doing, they destroy the Church. 'If Christ has not been raised, your faith is futile and you are still in your sins' (I Corinthians 15:17).

Here we meet the first christological problem: if Christ is present, not only as power, but in his person, how are we to think of this presence so that it does not violate this person? To be present means a particular time and place, i.e. to be there. Even as the risen one, Jesus Christ remains the man Jesus in time and space. Because Jesus Christ is man, he is present in time and space; because Jesus Christ is God, he is eternally present. The presence of Christ requires the statement, 'Jesus is fully man'; but it also requires the other statement, 'Jesus is fully God'. The presence of Jesus Christ in the Church, at a particular time and place, is because of the fact that there is one whole person of the God-Man. It is therefore an impossible question to ask how the man Jesus, limited by space and time, can be contemporary with us. This Jesus does not exist in isolation. Equally impossible is the other question, how God can be in time. This isolated God does not exist. The only possible and meaningful question is, 'Who is there, present in time and place?' The answer is, 'The one person of the God-Man, Jesus Christ'. I do not know who the man Jesus Christ is unless I can at the same time say, 'Jesus Christ is God'; I do not know who the God Jesus Christ is, unless I can at the same time say, 'Jesus Christ is man'. The two factors cannot be isolated, because they are not separable. God in timeless eternity is not God; Jesus limited by time is not Jesus. Rather we may say that in the man Jesus, God is God. In this Jesus Christ, God is present. This one God-Man is the starting point for christology.

The space-time continuum is not only the human definition of the God-Man, but also the divine definition. This space-time presence of the God-Man is hidden 'in the likeness of

45

sinful flesh' (Romans 8:3). The presence is a hidden presence. It is not that God is hidden in man, but rather that this God-Man as a whole is hidden in 'the likeness of sinful flesh'. That means that the principle of hiddenness is not man as such, not space and time, but the 'likeness of sinful flesh', i.e. the world between temptation and sin.

In this way the whole problem of christology is shifted. For here the issue is now that relationship between the already given God-Man and the 'likeness of sinful flesh', not a discussion on how to relate an isolated God to an isolated man in Christ. This God-Man, Jesus Christ, is present and contemporary in the form which is in the 'likeness of sinful flesh', i.e. in hidden form, in the form of a stumbling block. That is the central problem of christology.

The presence of the already given God-Man, Jesus Christ, is hidden from us, and exists in the offensive form of preaching. The Christ who is preached is the real Christ. The proclamation is not a second incarnation. The offence of Jesus Christ is not his incarnation – that indeed is revelation – but his humiliation. The humanity of Christ and the humiliation of Christ need to be distinguished with care. Jesus Christ is man both when he is humiliated and when he is exalted. Only the humiliation is an offence. The doctrine of the offence, the *scandalon*, is found not in the incarnation of God, but in the doctrine of the humiliated God-Man. It is the 'likeness of sinful flesh' which belongs to the humiliation. But for us that means that Christ is present as the risen and exalted one only in preaching; and that means only by way of a new humiliation. Thus, in proclamation, the risen and exalted one is present in his humiliation. This presence has a threefold form in the Church: that of the Word, that of the Sacrament, and that of the Congregation.

But the basic question of the presence of Christ is not yet answered. The question, 'How can the Man Jesus or the God Christ be present here and now?', is quite inadmissible. The fact of his presence is not in question. The question is really about the kind of structure of his person which enables Christ to be present in the Church.

If we answer, 'He is able because he is both God and Man', that is right, but it does not explain anything. The structure of his person must be outlined more clearly and unfolded as the *pro me* structure (that is, the structure I can relate to) of the God-Man, Jesus Christ. Christ is Christ, not just for himself, but in relation to me. His being Christ is his being for me, *pro me*. This being *pro me* is not to be understood as an effect emanating from him, nor as an accident; but it is to be understood as the essence, the being of the person himself. The core of the person himself is the *pro me*. That Christ is *pro me* is not an historical, nor an ontic statement, but an ontological one. Christ can never be thought of as being for himself, but only in relation to me. That in turn means that Christ can only be thought of existentially, or to put it another way, in the Church. Christ is not first a Christ for himself and then a Christ in the Church. He who alone is the Christ is the one who is present in the Church *pro me*. As Luther says, 'There is therefore a distinction between when God is there and when he is there for you' (Luther, *Weimarer Ausgabe* 23, 152). It is not only useless to contemplate a Christ for himself, it is even godless. It is this which makes intelligible Melancthon's defence in the *Loci*, which ends up in a repudiation of every christology. Every christology which does not begin with the assumption that God is only God for me, Christ is only Christ for me, condemns itself. Specific christological work can begin freely once this presupposition is accepted. Theology has often apostatized at this point. Either it has pushed its scholastic tendencies further and lost the concept of 'existence for you' in an independent existence; or it has looked only upon the acts and effects of Christ. But what is decisive about the *pro me* structure is that being and act of Christ are maintained together in it. *Actio Deo* and *praesentia Dei*, the *for you* existence and *being there* for you are joined together. When the unity of the act and being of Jesus Christ is understood in this way then the question of his person can be asked, i.e. the question of *who* he is. He is the one who has really bound himself in the freedom of his existence to me. And he is the one who has preserved his contingency freely in being there for me. He does not *have* the power of being for me, but he *is* the power.

The *pro me* structure means three things for the relation of Christ to the new humanity:

1. Jesus Christ *pro me* is the first fruits, the spearhead, the first-born of many brethren who follow him. The *pro me* structure is thus related to the historicity of Jesus. In the sense of first fruits for the others he is *pro me*.

2. Jesus Christ is for his brethren because he stands in their place. Christ stands for his new humanity before God. But if that is so, he is the new humanity. There where mankind should stand, he stands as a representative, enabled by his *pro me* structure. He is the Church. He not only acts for it, he is it, when he goes to the cross, carries the sins and dies. Therefore, in him, mankind is crucified, dead and judged.

3. Because he acts as the new humanity, it is in him and he in it. Because the new humanity is in him, God is gracious to it in him.

This one and complete person, the God-Man, Jesus Christ, is in the Church in his *pro me* structure as Word, as Sacrament and as Community.

This way of beginning christology with such a statement of his presence has the advantage that Jesus is understood from the beginning and already known as risen and ascended into heaven. The difficulty, however, consists of maintaining the unity of act and being; either Christ is there, in which case he is not essentially *pro me*, but even independent of me; or he is essentially *pro me* here, and in that case is he also apart from me there?

48

I. The Form of Christ

1. *Christ as Word*

1) Christ the Word is truth. There is no truth apart from the Word and by the Word. Spirit is originally word and speech, not power, feeling or act. 'In the beginning was the Word . . . and all things were made through the Word' (John 1:1, 3). Only as Word is the Spirit also power and act. God's Word creates and destroys. 'The Word of God is . . . sharper than a two-edged sword, piercing to the division' (Hebrews 4:12). God's Word carries the destroying lightning and the life-giving rain. As Word, it destroys and it creates the truth.

It is playing games to ask whether God is able to reveal himself in any other way than through the Word. Of course God has the freedom to reveal himself in other ways than we know. But God *has* revealed himself in the Word. He has bound himself to the Word that he might speak to men. He does not alter this Word.

2) Christ is the Word and not colour, shape or stone. It is for men that Christ is there as Word. Man is under the necessity of understanding the meaning of things. He is distinguished from the animals by the meaningfulness of his existence. Because man has a logos, God meets him in the Logos, who speaks and who is himself the Word. *Homo sapiens* speaks and that makes him *homo sapiens*. The Word conveys unambiguous and clear meaning. Clarity and simplicity are of its very nature. It is its own explanation. Clarity and simplicity are the reasons for its universal validity. Clarity and simplicity are of the very nature of the Word of God. The divine Logos is truth and meaning.

In Christ the divine Logos enters the human logos; that is the humiliation of Jesus Christ. One should be careful to note that God's Logos does not become identified with the human logos, as is assumed by German idealism, neither does it become analogous to it, as Catholicism teaches. Such misunderstandings lead to the idea of self-redemption and in this way the human logos escapes the judgement of the Christ Logos.

3) Christ as the Logos of God remains different and separate from the logos of men. He is the Word in the form of living address to men, but the word of men is word in the form of the idea. Address and idea are the basic structures of the word. But they exclude each other. Human thought is dominated by the form of the word as idea. The idea rests in itself and is related to itself; its validity holds throughout space and time. When Christ is called the Word of God today, it is usually with this sense of the idea. An idea is generally accessible, it lies ready to hand. Man can freely appropriate what he chooses from it. Christ as idea is timeless truth, the idea of God embodied in Jesus, available to anyone at any time.

The Word as address stands in contrast to all this. While it is possible for the Word as idea to remain by itself, as address it is only possible between two. Address requires response and responsibility. It is not timeless but happens in history. It does not rest and is not accessible to anyone at any time. It happens only when the address is made. The word lies wholly and freely at the disposal of the one who speaks. Thus it is unique and every time new. Its character as address requires the community. The character of truth in this addressing word is such that it seeks community, in order to face it with the truth. Truth is not something in itself, which rests for itself, but something that happens between two. Truth happens only in community. It is here for the first time that the concept of the Word acquires its full significance.

Christ as Word in the sense of address is thus not timeless truth. It is truth spoken into the concrete moment; it is address which places a man in the truth before God. It is not universally available idea, but Word, which is heard only when he allows it to be heard. It is not flesh and blood which reveals Christ, but the Father in heaven (Matthew 16:17) where and when he will.

Christ as Word in the sense of address is then also first really Christ *pro me*. Thus this definition of Christ as the addressing Word adequately expresses at one and the same time the contingency of revelation and its connection with men.

4) It is from these presuppositions that the content of the addressing Word is also defined. Its content is not the uncovering of hidden truths, nor the imparting of a new concept of God, nor a new moral teaching. It is far more concerned with the personal appeal of God to men to assume responsibility. Man in his being and existence is placed in the truth. Christ becomes the address of forgiveness and command. It does not matter whether the command is old or new – it can be either old or new – but what matters is that it happens. And also that forgiveness happens. But both forgiveness and command happen because the Word of God is the person of Christ.

5) The relation between word and person can be thought of in different ways. The person of Christ can be thought of as the bearer of an idea. He can be thought of as a prophet; a person through whom God speaks. He *says* the Word, but he *is* not it. That kind of thought concerns, not his person, but his task. The New Testament speaks firmly against this understanding. There Christ says of himself: 'I *am* the way and the truth and the life' (John 14:6). And this is declared as the only possibility of God's revelation, happening in him who does not *have* the Word in his person, but *is* the Word. He is the Word as the Son.

6) Christ is not only present *in* the Word of the Church, but also *as* Word of the Church, that means the spoken Word of preaching. *In* the Word, could be too little, because it could separate Christ from his Word. Christ's presence is his existence as proclamation. The whole Christ is present in

preaching, humiliated and exalted. His presence is not that power of the congregation or its objective spirit, out of which the preaching is made, but his existence as preaching. If that were not so, preaching could not have that prominent place which the Reformation insisted upon. This place belongs to the simplest sermon. The sermon is both the riches and the poverty of the Church. It is the form of the present Christ to which we are bound and to which we must hold. If the complete Christ is not in the preaching, then the Church is broken. The relation between God's Word and man's word in preaching is not that of mutual exclusion. The human word of preaching is not a phantom of the Word of God. Rather, God's Word has really entered into the humiliation of the words of men. Man's sermon is the Word of God, because God has freely bound himself and is bound to the words of men. Luther wrote, 'To this man should you point and say: there is God'. We would alter it slightly: 'To this word of man you should point and say: that is the Word of God'. Both statements are basically identical. One cannot point to this word of man without pointing to this man Jesus who is God.

So Christ is present in the Church as the spoken word, not as music nor as art. Present as the spoken word of judgement and forgiveness. Two things have to be said here with equal emphasis: I could not preach if I did not know that I spoke *the Word of God* – and: I could not preach if I did not know that *I* cannot say the Word of God. What is impossible for man and what God promises are the same.

2. *Christ as Sacrament*

Two things have to be said: Christ is wholly Word, and the sacrament also offers the full presence of the Word. Or to put it another way: the sacrament is to be distinguished from the Word and has a specific justification for its existence.

1) The sacrament is Word of God, because it is proclamation of the Gospel. It is not mystery or mute symbolic action, but

its action is consecrated and interpreted by the Word. The promise of the forgiveness of sins makes the sacrament what it is, clear revelation. Whoever believes the Word in the sacrament has the whole sacrament.

2) The Word in the sacrament is embodied Word. It is not representation of the Word. Only that which is not present can be represented. But the Word is present. The elements of water, bread and wine, given to us by name from God, become sacraments. It is because God's Word addresses them that they become corporeal forms of the sacrament, just as the creature first became creature when God addressed it by name. The word preached is the form in which the Logos reaches the human logos. The sacrament is the form in which the Logos reaches man in his nature. If we are to maintain that the object becomes what it is only when it has been named, we must note a distinction from philosophical conceptual realism. The fallen creation is no longer the creation of the first creative Word. The 'I' of man is no longer what God named, race no longer race, history no longer history. One sees the Word no longer in creation. The continuity of Word and nature is lost. The creation is not sacrament. There is sacrament only when God, by his special Word, in the midst of his created world, addresses, names and hallows an element.

Thus the Eucharist is what it is only because God, by his Word, addresses and hallows the elements of bread and wine. This Word is called Jesus Christ. The sacrament is both interpreted and hallowed by Jesus Christ. God has bound himself to these elements by this Word, Jesus Christ, addressed to the sacrament. This Word, Jesus Christ, is completely present in the Sacrament, neither his Godhead alone, nor only his humanity.

3) It is true also in the sacrament that Jesus Christ is God's spoken Word. But against the attempt to limit Christ to doctrine, or to lose him in general truth, the Church stresses the sacramental form of Christ. He is not only doctrine, nor

only idea, but nature and history. The inadequacies of nature and history are God's cloak. But not everything corporeal, not all nature and history, is meant to be sacramental. Nature as such does not symbolize Christ. His presence is confined to the forms of preaching and the two sacraments.

Why these sacraments in particular? Protestant teaching says, because they are instituted by Jesus himself. But this is not to be understood simply in an historical sense. 'Instituted by Jesus' cannot mean other than given to his Church by the exalted and present Christ. The number of sacraments in which Christ is present is determined simply by the fact that they were instituted by the exalted Lord, i.e. positivistically. Thus narrowly and positively defined they do not stand as symbols for something else, but they are Word of God. They do not *interpret* something, they *are* it.

4) The sacrament is not a concealment of the incorporeal Word of God under the cover of a bodily form, so that one might think of the sacrament as a second incarnation. But the incarnate one, who has become flesh and blood, is in the sacrament as the stumbling block. The sacrament is not God becoming man, but the humiliation of the God-Man. This is analogous to what was said earlier, that the primary question in christology is not about the possibility of uniting deity and humanity, but rather about the concealment of the God-Man in his humiliation. God is revealed in the flesh, but concealed in the stumbling block. It follows, therefore, that the question about the presence of Christ in the sacrament may not be posed or analysed as a question about the humanity and deity of Christ, but only as the question of the presence of the God-Man in the form of his humiliation or offence.

5) A labyrinth of misunderstanding arose in protestant theology, because of false questioning. The question was related on the one hand to the possibility of a presence of the humanity of Christ in the sacrament, and on the other hand to

the relationship between Christ's *existence* and his being *for me*.

That Christ will be present in the Church as man, he has said in the words of institution of the Eucharist. Luther would not have these words undermined. He clung to the recognition that the man Jesus must be present if any good is to come to us from the work of Christ. Everything comes from the presence of the man Jesus Christ, here and now. Therefore, for Luther, the whole Gospel depended upon the words of institution of Jesus.

That was opposed by the protest that Jesus Christ was the one who had ascended into heaven. The Reformers asked how it could be possible for the one who sits at the right hand of God to be present, here and now. At first, Luther made a joke of this question, saying that they must not try to confine God to a limited space, like the bird in the nest (*Weimarer Ausgabe* 23, 158). The Reformed theologians argued that Christ, as the person of the Logos, during the sacrament, existed outside the corporeal state. The Logos was not confined to his corporeal state, but also remained outside it. This doctrine of the *Extra-Calvinisticum* is the result of asking the question, 'How?' But Lutheran theology allowed the question to be posed. Luther answered it with the doctrine of ubiquity. The body of Jesus, as the body of the God-Man, had taken upon itself divine properties through its *communicatio* with the divine nature. This body of Jesus Christ is not bound by space, but is present in all places at the same time, due to the *genus majestaticum*. The transfigured body is present everywhere; and so too, therefore, is Christ's humanity present in the Eucharist.

Luther knows three different modes of presence:
a) *localiter* or *circumscriptive*, as when in his earthly life the body of Jesus Christ was there to be circumscribed (*W.A.* 26, 337);
b) *diffinitive*, like the angels and demons, who are everywhere

and yet appear in a particular place (*W.A.* 26, 328);

c) *repletive*, when something is everywhere and yet cannot in any way be measured or defined (*W.A.* 26, 329).

In this third way, described under c), Jesus Christ is now present, according to Luther – i.e. everywhere and yet intangible. He is *in* the bread, but not as straw is in a sack; this *in* must be understood theologically. He is only there, where he reveals himself in his Word. 'It has only to do with revelation. He is present everywhere, but you will not be able to grasp him, unless he offers himself to you and explains the bread to you, by his Word. You will not eat him unless he wishes to reveal himself to you' (Luther, *W.A.* 19, 492; 23, 151). Christ is also in the rustling leaves, as Luther says, but he is not there *for you*, i.e. he is not manifest.

What christological significance do these statements have? Here christology has become *Eucharistic Christology*. Its thought is governed by the Eucharist. But Luther has answered the question, 'How?' Luther dealt with the question of how Christ is present by means of two different doctrines: with the doctrine of *ubiquity* (he is present everywhere) and the doctrine of the *ubivoli* presence (he is only present for you when he wishes to be there for you). As metaphysical hypostases, both doctrines are impossible. In each, an element of reality has been isolated and elevated into a system. Neither statement is right for what it has to describe. The statement that Christ is ubiquitous passes over his existence as a person; the statement that his presence is where he wills, *in actu*, understands his presence not as a mode of existence, but, in the manner of Chemnitz, as an accident of the person.

Equal regard must be paid to Christ's being there and his being for you. The doctrine of ubiquity teaches a Christ outside revelation; revelation becomes the accident of a substance already there. The doctrine of the *ubivoli* presence teaches Christ as being present, not in terms of a particular person, but as a promise bound up with the word of Jesus.

Neither doctrine understands the *pro me* presence of Christ as his own mode of existence. They are both theologically inadequate because they cannot give appropriate expression to the presence of the God-Man, the person who is the one both exalted and humiliated. They answer the question, 'How?', and lead necessarily into a conceptual blind alley. They were the result of questions put by the Reformed churches on Lutheran soil and they brought great confusion to later Lutheran theology. Nevertheless, the blind alleys of their understanding are better and more factual than the rationalist simplifications of Schlcicrmacher, who adjusted the facts to fit the question, 'How?'

6) The question of the presence of Christ in the sacrament cannot be answered from the question, 'How?' '*Who* is present in the sacrament?', is the only question to ask. 'The complete person of the God-Man is present, in his exaltation and humiliation', is the answer. Christ exists in such a way that he is existentially present in the sacrament. His being in the sacrament is not a special property, one quality among others; this is the way in which he exists in the Church. The humiliation is no accident of his divine-human substance, but it is his existence.

Is there a Christ of the sacrament and a Christ of preaching? Is the one who is present in the sacrament different from the one who is present in the Word? No! He is the one judging and forgiving Christ, who is the Word, in both. In the Word he makes use of our human logos; in the sacrament he makes use of our body and is present in the sphere of tangible nature. In the sacrament, Christ is by our side as creature, among us, brother with brother. But, even as creature, he is also the new creation. In the sacrament he breaks through the fallen creation at a defined point. He is the new creature. He is the restored creation of our spiritual and bodily existence.

He is the Word of God which has become bread and wine. As new creature he is in bread and wine. Thus bread and wine are a new creation. They are really nourishment for the new being. As elements of the restored creation they are not for themselves, but for men. This being-for-men is what makes them a new creation.

The Christ present in the sacrament is the creator of this new creation and at the same time a creature. He is present as our creator, who makes us into new creatures. But he is also present as the humiliated creature in the sacrament and in no other way. Thus is he present.

The question of *how* this can be must be changed into the question, 'Who is this person who is thus present?' The answer is, the historical and crucified, the risen one, who has ascended into heaven, the God-Man revealed as brother and Lord, as creature and creator.

3. *Christ as Church*

Just as Christ is present as Word and in the Word, as sacrament and in the sacrament, so he is also present as Church and in the Church. His presence in Word and sacrament is related to his presence in the Church as reality is related to form. Christ is the Church by virtue of his *pro me* being. Between his ascension and his coming again the Church is his form and indeed his only form. That he is in heaven at the right hand of God does not contradict this; on the contrary, this is what makes possible his presence in and as the Church.

What does it mean that Christ as *Word* is also Church? It means that the Logos of God has existence in space and time in and as the Church. Christ the Word is spiritually and bodily present. The Logos is not merely the weak word of human teaching, *doctrina*, but it is the powerful Word of the Creator. He speaks and thereby creates the form of the Church. The Church is thus not only receiver of the Word of revelation, but is itself revelation and Word of God. Only in so far as it is itself Word of God, can it understand the Word of God. Revelation can be understood only on the basis of revelation.

The Word is *in* the Church in so far as the Church is the recipient of revelation. But the Word is also itself Church, in so far as the Church itself is revelation and the Word wishes to have the form of a created body.

What does it mean that Christ as *sacrament* is also Church? Christ as sacrament is also in the Church and is the Church. The sacrament has already the bodily form in itself which goes beyond that of the Word. The Church is the body of Christ. Here body is not only a symbol. The Church *is* the body of Christ, it does not *signify* the body of Christ. When applied to the Church, the concept of body is not only a concept of function, which refers only to the members of this body. It is a comprehensive and central concept of the mode of existence of the one who is present in his exaltation and humiliation.

This Christ existing as Church is the whole person, the one who is exalted and who is humiliated. His being as Church, like as with Word and sacrament, has the form of a stumbling block. In so far as it is Church, it is no longer in sin. But it remains in the world of the old Adam, in the 'likeness of sinful flesh', under the age of sin. It remains human in repentance (see I John).

Christ is not only the head of the Church, but also the Church itself (see I Corinthians 12 and Ephesians). Christ is head and also every member. It is first in Ephesians that we have the separation between head and members. That idea is not originally Pauline. Head means to be Lord. But the two views can be taken together and do not contradict one another.

II. The Place of Christ

When we ask about the place of Christ, we are asking about the '*Where?*' of Christ within the structure of the '*Who?*' So far, we remain within the structure of the person. It all depends upon Christ being present to his Church as person in space and time. If this structure can be shown to be of the essence of his nature and not fortuitous, accidental, then there will be theological proof that space and time is the way of existence of the person of the risen one. It is for this reason that we must ask about the 'Where?'

Where does he stand? He stands *pro me*. He stands there in my place, where I should stand, but cannot. He stands on the boundary of my existence, beyond my existence, yet for me. That brings out clearly that I am separated from my 'I', which I should be, by a boundary which I am unable to cross. The boundary lies between me and me, the old and the new 'I'. It is in the encounter with this boundary that I shall be judged. At this place, I cannot stand alone. At this place stands Christ, between me and me, the old and the new existence. Thus Christ is at one and the same time, my boundary and my rediscovered centre. He is the centre, between 'I' and 'I', and between 'I' and God. The boundary can only be known as boundary from beyond the boundary. In Christ, man recognizes it and thereby at the same time finds his new centre again.

It is the nature of the person of Christ to be in the centre, both spatially and temporally. The one who is present in Word, Sacrament and Church is in the centre of human existence, of history and of nature. It belongs to the structure of his person to be in the centre. When we turn the question, 'Where?', back into the question, 'Who?', we get the answer. Christ is the mediator as the one who exists *pro me*. That is his nature and his mode of existence. In three ways, he is in the centre: in being there for men, in being there for history, in being there for nature.

1. *Christ as the Centre of Human Existence*

That Christ is the centre of our existence does not mean that he is central in our personality, our thinking and our feeling. Christ is also our centre when he stands, in terms of our consciousness, on our periphery, also when Christian piety is displaced to the periphery of our being. The statement made about his centrality is not psychological, but has the character of an ontological and theological statement. It does not refer to our personality, but to our being a person before God. The centre of the person cannot be demonstrated. The truth of the statement that Christ is our centre does not allow of confirmation by proof. For it concerns the centre in which we believe within the space of the person in whom we believe.

In the fallen world the centre is also the boundary. Man stands between law and fulfilment. He has the law, but he cannot fulfil it. Now Christ stands where man has failed before the law. Christ as the centre means that he is the fulfilment of the law. So he is in turn the boundary and judgement of man, but also the beginning of his new existence, its centre. Christ as the centre of human existence means that he is the judgement and justification of man.

2. *Christ as the Centre of History*

Every attempt to give a philosophical basis for the fact that Christ is the centre of history must be rejected. There can be no question of proving that he is the centre and consummation of religious and secular history. Here too it is not a matter of finding the centre of historical space. Were Christ shown to be the high point of all religion, that would still have nothing to do with his being the centre. A comparison with other relative appearances and, resulting from that, a possible proof that Christ was the centre of history would at the most give us a relative, not an absolute conclusion. All questions about his absolute claim are wrongly stated. Comparisons with relative objects and conclusions to relative questions do not result in an absolute. The question about absolute claims is a liberal and rationalistic question and only serves to distort the question which is appropriate here. The question about Christ as centre and boundary of history must be stated quite differently.

History lives between promise and fulfilment. It carries the promise within itself, to become full of God, the womb of the birth of God. The promise of a Messiah is everywhere alive in history. History lives in and from this expectation. That is what gives it significance, the coming of the Messiah. But history relates itself to this promise much as the individual man relates to the law: it cannot fulfil it. The promise is corrupted by sin. Man has the law only in the corrupted form sin itself has caused. History has the promise only as it is corrupted in itself. It lives from the corrupted promises of 'fulfilled time', from its *kairos*. It must always make visible its own centre. In this situation it is forced to glory in its own messiahs. A messiah at the centre of history is, from the point of view of the philosophy of history, quite a respectable theory. But this promise remains unfulfilled. History is tormented by the impossibility of fulfilling corrupt messianic promises. It knows of its messianic determination and comes to grief on it.

Only at one point does the thought break through that the Messiah cannot be the visible and demonstrated centre of history, but must be the hidden centre appointed by God. This is the point at which there is a stream against the popular movement of corrupted messianism – it is in Israel. With its prophetic hope, it stands alone among the nations. And Israel becomes the place at which God fulfils his promise.

This fulfilled promise is not to be proved by anything, it is only to be proclaimed. This means that the Messiah, Christ, is at one and the same time the destroyer and the fulfiller of all the messianic expectations of history. He is the destroyer in so far as the visible Messiah does not appear and the fulfilment takes place in secret. He is the fulfiller in so far as God really enters history and he who is expected is really there. The meaning of history is tied up with an event which takes place in the depth and hiddenness of a man who ended on the cross. The meaning of history is found in the humiliated Christ.

With this every other claim of history is judged and settled. History is here led to its boundary with its own promises. By its nature it has come to an end. Yet, by setting this boundary,

THE PRESENT CHRIST — THE PRO ME

Christ has at the same time again become its centre and its fulfilment. When the totality of history should stand before God, there Christ stands. He is also the *pro me* for history. He is also the mediator for history.

Because Christ, since the cross and resurrection, is present in the Church, the Church also must be understood as the centre of history. It is the centre of a history which is being made by the state. Again this is a hidden and not an evident centre of the realm of the state. The Church does not show itself to be the centre by visibly standing at the centre of the state or by letting itself be put at the centre, as when it is made a state Church. It is not its visible position in the realm of the state that shows its relation to the state. The meaning and the promise of the state is hidden in it, it judges and justifies the state in its nature. Its nature, i.e. the nature of the state, is to bring a people nearer to its fulfilment by law and the order it creates. With the thought of an order-creating state, that messianic claim dwells hidden within.

So, just as the Church is the centre of the state, it is also its boundary. It is the boundary of the state in proclaiming with the cross the breaking-through of all human order. Just as it recognizes and believes in the cross, as the fulfilment of the law, so it also believes the cross to be the fulfilment of the order of the state. When it recognizes the cross and proclaims it, the Church does not judge by a new law, according to which the state would have to act. But it proclaims that by God's entry into history and his death through history, the order of the state has been finally broken through and dissolved, but also finally affirmed and fulfilled.

Therefore the relationship of Church and state since the cross is new. There is a state, in the proper sense, only when there is a Church. The state has its proper origin since and with the cross (like the Church) in so far as this cross destroys and fulfils and affirms its order.

Christ is present to us in the forms both of Church and

State. But he is this only for us, who receive him as Word and Sacrament and Church; for us, who since the cross must see the state in the light of Christ. The state is God's 'rule with his left hand' (Luther, *W.A.* 36, 385, 6-9; 52, 26, 20-6). So long as Christ was on earth, he was the kingdom of God. When he was crucified the kingdom broke up into one ruled by God's right hand and one ruled by his left hand. Now, it can only be recognized in a twofold form, as Church and as State. But the complete Christ is present in his Church. And this Church is the hidden centre of the state. The state need not know that the Church is this centre, but in fact it lives from this centre and has no effective existence without it.

Christ as centre of history is the mediator between state and God in the form of the Church. In the same way, he is as centre of history also mediator between Church and God. He is also the centre of this Church, only so can it be the centre of history.

3. *Christ as the Centre Between God and Nature*

There has been little consideration of this question in Protestant theology in the past.

Christ is *the* new creature. Thereby he shows all other creatures to be old creatures. Nature stands under the curse which God laid upon Adam's ground. It was the originally created Word of God, proclaiming it freely. As the fallen creation it is now dumb, enslaved under the guilt of man. Like history, it suffers from the loss of its meaning and its freedom. It waits expectantly for a new freedom. Nature, unlike man and history, will not be reconciled, but it will be set free for a new freedom. Its catastrophes are the dull will to set itself free, to show its power over man and by its own right to be a new creature, which it has made anew itself.

In the sacrament of the Church, the old enslaved creature is set free to its new freedom. As the centre of human existence and of history, Christ was the fulfilment of the unfulfilled law, i.e. their reconciliation. But nature is creation under the curse – not guilt, for it lacks freedom. Thus nature finds in Christ as its centre, not reconciliation, but redemption. Once again, this redemption, which happens in Christ, is not evident, nor can it be proved, but it is proclaimed. The word of preaching is that enslaved nature is redeemed in hope. A sign of this is given in the sacraments, where elements of the old creation are become elements of the new. In the sacraments they are set free from their dumbness and proclaim directly to the believer the new creative Word of God. They no longer need the explanation of man. Enslaved nature does not speak the Word of God to us directly. But the sacraments do. In the sacrament, Christ is the mediator between nature and God and stands for all creation before God.

To sum up, we must continue to emphasize that Christ is truly the centre of human existence, the centre of history and now also the centre of nature. But these three aspects can only be distinguished from each other *in abstracto*. In fact, human existence is also and always history, always and also nature. The mediator as fulfiller of the law and liberator of creation is all this for the whole of human existence. He is the same who is intercessor and *pro me*, and who is himself the end of the old world and the beginning of the new world of God.

PART TWO

THE HISTORICAL CHRIST

I. Approach to the Historical Christ

The present Christ of whom we have spoken so far is the historical Christ. But this historical Christ is Jesus of Nazareth in history. If it were not so, then what Paul said in another context would be true, our faith is futile and an illusion. The substance of the Church would be removed. One must understand that the isolation of the so-called Jesus of history from the present Christ and vice versa is a fiction.

The attempt of liberal theology to distinguish between the Jesus of the Synoptic Gospels and the Pauline Christ is doomed to failure, judged both historically and dogmatically. Dogmatically: if this separation of Jesus from Christ were possible, the preaching of the Church would be an illusion. Historically: until about 1900, liberal theology can be described as an indirect, unintentional and therefore all the more impressive, confirmation of the need for a dogmatic support. The results of liberal theology are its own destruction. They make room for the assertion, which they sought to deny, that Jesus is the Christ.

Liberal theology stands or falls with the separation of Jesus from Christ. The Christ is Jesus who has been enthusiastically divinized by the Church. It is not in his being nor in his person that Jesus is the Christ, but in his effect upon others. Thus, according to the liberal theologians, Jesus himself in his being must be distinguished from Jesus in the opinion of the Church. Hence came the studies on 'Jesus of History' and the 'lives' of Jesus. Scientific research must uncover the historical Jesus and dispose of the Jesus who is the Christ. The results were unexpected. It was liberal theology itself which was disposed of by this undertaking! It was not possible to write an historically credible life of Jesus. Books appeared by Wrede and Schweitzer (W. Wrede, *Uber Aufgabe und Methode der sogenannte neutestamentlichen Theologie*, 1897 and *Das Messiasgeheimnis in den Evangelium*, 1901; A. Schweitzer, *The Quest of the Historical Jesus*, 1906). Schweitzer came to the conclusion that the quest for the historical Jesus is in itself an impossibility. Wrede makes quite clear that an historical Jesus in the sense of these researches into the life of Jesus is not feasible, because the Synoptic Gospels are written already under the presupposition of the 'faith of the Church'. One cannot get behind belief in the Christ as Lord (*Kyrios Christos*).

The end of liberal theology had a double significance: a) Negative: the destruction of its presupposition that Jesus is other than the Christ.

b) Positive: from now on, the New Testament can only be rightly interpreted *historically*, when the presupposition that Jesus is already proclaimed Christ, as Lord, is taken seriously.

There remain two ways open, either to keep on the historical level, despite all that has been said, and to place this *Kyrios Christos* cult beside other similar cults, or to try to find a bridge between the historical level and dogmatic study. The historical level has shown that Jesus cannot be separated from the Christ. A Jesus religion in which only the Father plays a role, and a cult of Christ, can no longer be set up in opposition to each other. And therefore a theology which sets out from this idea has also become impossible. This result is the more surprising since dogmatic and historical studies have appeared to be opposed from the beginning. It was with Wrede that the covenant between history and dogmatics was finally renewed. History has reworked the presuppositions of dogmatics in the New Testament and come upon the unity of the present and the historical Christ, of the Jesus proclaimed and the Jesus of history.

Martin Kähler, in his book *Der sogenannte historische Jesus und der geschichtliche biblische Jesus,* 1892, laid down two axioms:

a) The quest of the historical Jesus is a blind alley.

b) The Christ who is preached is the historical Christ.

Dogmatics was thus saying what historical theology later acknowledged. Now comes the time when dogmatic interest lies less in seeking to understand the divine influence of Jesus and more in understanding the deity of Jesus Christ.

But what happens if at a later stage historical study again throws doubt upon the dogmatic statements, perhaps even makes them impossible, because its conclusions have changed again? How far are these dogmatic statements dependent upon historical support?

Two things must be said:

a) Dogmatics needs to be certain of the historicity of Jesus Christ, i.e. the identity of what is proclaimed with that which happened in history.

b) The question is how dogmatics can be certain of this historicity.

Can history bear the dogmatic statements? Is it possible to approach the historical figure of Jesus through history alone? If so, history would have to be regarded as *historia sacra* (sacred history). But that will not do, neither empirically nor theologically. Or is there a direct, non-historical approach to Jesus Christ? Or to put the question differently, how can the Church be absolutely sure of the historical fact?

It belongs to the nature of historical study that it never reckons the individual fact to be absolute. It can never base everything upon the individual fact. Every individual fact has something of chance in it. Its absolute necessity can never be demonstrated after the event. But now, the fact, historically the chance fact, of the life and death of Jesus must be fundamental and of absolute significance for the Church. If he has not lived, the Church is doomed. If the Church is not sure of this, it is finished. How then can it be sure of the historical fact of 'Jesus Christ'? Here, clearly, historical research and its methods are superseded. This is how we must answer these questions:

a) Historical research can never absolutely deny, because it can never absolutely affirm. Absolute denial or absolute affirmation make history into *historia sacra*. So the existence of Jesus Christ cannot be absolutely denied. Historical study can only put it in doubt or make it improbable. As a subject for historical investigation, Jesus Christ remains an uncertain phenomenon; his historicity can neither be affirmed nor denied with the necessary absolute certainty. Thus it cannot with absolute authority be said that dogmatic statements are impossible.

b) Absolute certainty about an historical fact is in itself never attainable. It remains a paradox. Nevertheless it remains essential for the Church. That means that for the Church the historical fact is not in the past, but present; that the uncertain is the absolute, the past is the present and the historical is contemporary (Kierkegaard). Only when this paradox can be born is the historical, absolute. This statement that the historical becomes contemporary, the hidden revealed, is only possible when it has itself become contemporary and revealed, i.e. in faith in God's miracle of the resurrection of Jesus Christ.

There is no way from history to the absolute. There is no absolute ground for faith derived from history. But from where does faith receive its sufficient ground to know that the uncertain is sure? There is only the witness of the risen one to himself, by which the Church bears witness to him as 'in history'. By the miracle of his presence in the Church, he bears witness to himself as there in history, here and now.

The historical approach to the Jesus of history is not binding for the believer. Historical certainty is not a union with Jesus; that is no more than encounter with any other person from the past. We can have 'Moments with Christ' as we can with Goethe. It is not a mystical union either with some person in history, but rather a person who bears witness to himself. Neither is it what Wilhelm Herrmann describes as the bewildered conscience finding an encounter with Jesus in the inner life and by this encounter forming a conviction of the figure of Jesus in history. But it is the risen one who himself creates faith and thus knows the way to himself 'in history'. When we have Christ witnessing to himself in the present, any historical confirmation is irrelevant. In faith, history is known, not from within nor from itself, but in the light of eternity. This is the direct approach of faith to history.

But does this not open the door to every kind of sentimentality? Such is not the case, because the witness of Jesus Christ to himself is none other than that which the Scriptures deliver to us and which comes to us by no other way than by the Word of the Scriptures. We are first concerned with a book which we find in the secular sphere. It must be read and interpreted. It will be read with all the help possible from historical and philosophical criticism. Even the believer has to do this with care and scholarship. Occasionally we have to deal with a problematic situation; perhaps we have to preach about a text, which we know from scholarly criticism was never spoken by Jesus. In the exegesis of Scripture we find ourselves on thin ice. One can never stand firm at one point, but must move about over the whole of the Bible. As we move from one place to another we are like a man crossing a river covered in ice floes, who does not remain standing on one particular piece of ice, but jumps from one to another (Thurneysen).

There may be some difficulties about preaching from a text whose authenticity has been destroyed by historical research. Verbal inspiration is a poor substitute for the resurrection! It amounts to a denial of the unique presence of the risen one. It gives history an eternal value instead of seeing history and knowing it from the point of view of God's eternity. It is wrecked in its attempt to level the rough ground. The Bible remains a book like other books. One must be ready to accept the concealment within history and therefore let historical criticism run its course. But it is through the Bible, with all its flaws, that the risen one encounters us. We must get into the troubled waters of historical criticism. Its importance is not absolute, but neither is it unimportant. Certainly it will not lead to a weakening, but rather to a strengthening of faith, because the concealment within the historical belongs to the humiliation of Christ.

The historical nature of Jesus Christ has two aspects, that of history and that of faith. Both aspects are bound together. The Jesus of history has humbled himself; the Jesus who cannot be grasped by history is the one to whom resurrection faith is directed.

In what follows, the historical form of the risen one will be considered. The early Church began with the Jesus Christ of history and gave little attention to the present and risen Christ. They took this for granted. But we have lost this self-evident assumption. So we have to be concerned here first with his presence.

II. Critical or Negative Christology

Here we are concerned with that part of christology in which the incomprehensibility of the person of Christ should be made comprehensible. Yet, wisdom should leave the incomprehensible as it is. The incomprehensible cannot be changed into something comprehensible; we shall rather concern ourselves with resisting every attempt to make that change. *Critical christology* has as its objective the delimiting of what must be placed within the category of the incomprehensible. It will therefore be critical, because it will test every statement about Christ with regard to these limits. The results of critical christology are of a negative kind, because they determine the boundaries and establish the rules for what may *not* be said about Christ.

Positive christology can be developed from there. The attempt of a positive christology must again and again be subject to criticism. This is demonstrated in history by the fact that the Councils always produced a negative, delimiting christology as a result of their deliberations. The movements towards a positive christology, on the other hand, were pioneered by individual theologians. The Councils gave these attempts their critical limits, beyond which they may not proceed. These conciliar contributions are the content of critical theology. Positive theology served the Councils by forcing them to define these limits ever more sharply. The progress from Council to Council was occasioned by those men who had appeared in the interval and pushed forward positive christology. Critical christology is a matter for the official Church, it has its place in the authoritative teaching of the Councils. Positive christology persists and happens actually in the proclamation of the Church and has its place in the preaching and the sacraments. The limits fixed by the early Church are shown in our day to have tremendous significance.

If critical christology is concerned with the fixing of limits, that means it is concerned with the concept of heresy. The concept of heresy is lost today because there is no longer a teaching authority. This is a terrible decline. The present-day ecumenical councils are everything but Councils, because the word 'heresy' is struck out from their vocabulary. There can be no credal confession without saying, 'In the light of Christ, this is true and this is false!' The concept of heresy belongs necessarily and irrevocably with the concept of a credal confession. The teaching of a Confessing Church must stand in opposition to a false teaching. The Augsburg Confession says quite clearly, 'The Church condemns'.

It must here be noted that the concept of heresy emerges from the fellowship of the Church and not from an absence of love. Only when man does not withhold the truth from his brother, does he deal with him in a brotherly way. If I do not tell him the truth, then I treat him like a heathen. When I speak the truth to one who is of a different opinion from mine, then I offer him the love I owe him.

1. *The Docetic Heresy* (*Liberal Theology*)

The docetic heresy attempts to make the incarnation of Christ comprehensible by understanding Jesus Christ as a manifestation of the deity in history. Christ's manhood is a cloak and a veil; it is a means God uses to speak to men. But it does not belong to the essence of the matter. Jesus the man is the transparent cloak for God. This heresy is as old as Christianity itself. It lives still in the present. It draws its strength from two sources:

a) From an abstract idea of God. That is a teaching about God which can take no regard of man and defines his nature without reference to him. One knows the deity already before he is revealed. One knows the truth already as a suprahistorical, absolute idea. When God is thought of as an idea, Christ must be understood as an appearance of this idea, but not as an individual. This heresy disregards the humanity in Christ. If God wishes to encounter man, he leaves the world of ideas and enters the world of appearance. The form he chooses is unimportant compared with the core. The origin of this way of thinking lies in the Greek antithesis between idea and phenomenon. What appears in the world is inessential compared with what exists in the world of ideas. The docetic heresy is the typical heresy of Greek thought. It is a superb example of pagan thought. Its opposite is Jewish thought. In this there is no presupposition of an antithesis between idea and phenomenon, and thus docetism finds no place in it. Instead, the Ebionite heresy developed.

b) One particular view of redemption underlies the docetic heresy. In the early Church it was said that the nature of man must be redeemed by Christ. The individual man in his individuality is fallen. Schelling's words are, 'Individuality is sin'. According to this way of thinking, the particular man must be restored by release from his imprisonment in his individuality to his essence. This essence is the same for all men. Redemption is liberation from individuality and back to nature. This redemption re-establishes the unity and original state of the whole human race. 'Man, become what you are!' (Angelus Silesius). What Silesius said in those words, the early Church had already said and Idealism was later to say. Now when the Bible spoke of Christ's becoming man in order to be the Redeemer, docetic presuppositions took that to mean that God had taken the essence and nature of man, but not man with his individuality. By taking the nature of man, he redeemed him to his original nature, from the individuality, which is sin. But this raises the question of how one can talk of a full incarnation when God has taken the 'nature' of man, but not his individuality. This emphatic omission was to preserve God from the sin of individuality, which would have made redemption impossible.

This set the scene for the teaching of *Apollinarius of Laodicea*. He was one of the most brilliant and successful theologians of the early Church. He taught that while the Logos had certainly taken upon him the nature of man, with *sarx* and *psyche*, he had not taken the *nous*. What was understood there by the *nous* was that which made men into individuals, persons with cultural individuality. The incarnation is then an appearance of God in human nature, without the covering of individuality which belongs to this nature. The *nous* falls out of Jesus and its place is taken by the Logos. The full incarnation of God did not take place. This is a *dokein* (Greek, 'to seem' as opposed to reality). This subtle docetism was soon detected and the teaching of Apollinarius was condemned as heretical. It was an incomplete incarnation and therefore no incarnation at all, thus putting the redemption in question. The early Church recognized rather that the incarnate had taken *sarx, psyche* and *nous* (Greek, 'flesh', 'self' and 'mind').

As soon as this was safeguarded the problem arose as to *how* this individual person could be God. Could the full unity of person in Christ still be preserved? Is there not then in the incarnation a Jesus *and* a Christ? Although the old orthodoxy in the course of christological discussion had recognized the *nous* in Christ, it had difficulty with the thought that a Jesus – not only in his nature, but – in fallen individuality could be meant. They found a way out by shifting the problem. Although the incarnation was so taught that *sarx, psyche* and *nous* appeared to be held together, Jesus was not assigned his own *hypostasis* (later Greek, 'the special characteristic nature of a person', used to translate the Latin *persona*). He had no mode of existence of his own, but his existence was the existence of God. This is what was meant by the doctrine of *enhypostasia*. God and man were again separated, each into his own *hypostasis*. So the person of Jesus is to be enhypostatized with the hypostasis of God. But with this doctrine of *enhypostasia*, which was intended to prevent the falling apart of Christ into God and man, the theologians of the early Church found themselves fighting a rearguard action with docetism. This had slipped into the dogmatic teaching of the early Church in a subtle form once again. In its denial of the *hypostasis*, docetism had retreated to a secure position and held it. Brunner overlooks this in 'The Mediator', when he approves the doctrine of *enhypostasia* as a good insight of the early Church and adopts it. Luther has no such illusion: 'You should look upon the whole man, Jesus, and say, That is God!'

The reason why early christologies are so often deflected into docetism is tied up with the differentiation in man of his nature (essence) and his characteristic person (individuality) which we find in all thought about redemption. The abstract doctrine of God and the thought about redemption have the same presuppositions – that antithesis we have already mentioned between idea and phenomenon. The idea is substance; the phenomenon is accident. Christ, the God, is substance; Jesus, the man, is accident. It is a philosophical presupposition which has minted the docetic doctrine of the incarnation. He who does not free himself from this presupposition (Idea-Phenomenon) will seek in vain to escape from a crude or subtle form of docetism.

The original form of docetism is represented by the Gnostics, Basilides and Valentinus.

Basilides teaches that no union took place between the only-begotten Christ (*primogenitus nous*) and the phenomenon Jesus. Jesus was only the 'accidental' basis for the Christ, the union was only transitory and already dissolved before the crucifixion. Christ returned to heaven before the crucifixion and laughed at the devil. Jesus was a real man and the accidental starting point for the 'aeon' of Christ. *Valentinus* and his disciple *Apelles* teach that the body of Christ was not humanly born, but was a heavenly body. He simply went through Mary. *Satornil* goes so far as to say that Christ never had a body, he was not born and that he only appeared to suffer. All three have this in common, that they are quite indifferent to Jesus. He is the incidental appearance. What matters and what must be grasped is the idea and its unfolding. Whether it was Jesus in whom the idea was unfolded, and who Jesus was, does not matter.

The early Church opposed these docetists with all its strength. It was concerned to proclaim a happening and not an idea of redemption, and it held fast to the incarnation. The real man had to be redeemed. It staked everything on the historicity of Jesus Christ. Nevertheless, attempts were made to bring the historicity of this Jesus Christ into harmony with prevailing ideas of God and redemption. For this, modifications were needed. Eventually, after the Church's struggle with docetism, the legacy of *enhypostasia* remained. Its doctrine remained in the 'dogmatics' of the early Church as a tribute to the presuppositions of docetic thinking. Finally the incarnation was still thought of in its theological formulations as an accident of the substance. For all this, the enemy had been detected and named by name. Docetism was condemned as a deviation.

In more recent protestant theology, docetism has appeared again, but of course in a different form. There is now an interest in the historical Jesus. Where once there was a speculative idea of God, there is now a speculative concept of history. Now history is the support of particular religious ideas and values. History is now the manifestation of supra-historical ideas. One of these values is the idea of the religious personality of man with the 'continuing power of his consciousness of God' (Schleiermacher, *The Christian Faith*, p. 94). Jesus is the embodiment or the support for this idea in history. Why is that docetic? Because one has taken a particular religious idea in advance and then proceeded to apply it to the historical Jesus. In this way, a particular concept of history gives us an image of man and this we project upon Jesus. What is decisive (in coming to the conclusion that this is docetic) is that the incarnation has become a means to an end.

This is also clearly true of the christology of *Albrecht Ritschl*. He says that Christ is designated God only by the value judgement of the Church. The Church addresses him as such. By this judgement, Christ is God. Ritschl distinguishes judgements of being from judgements of value. The Church has a system of values. With this system, it approaches the figure of the historical Jesus, applies it to him or finds it realized in him. Such values embodied in Jesus are, among others, grace, faithfulness, lordship over the world. The man Jesus is the manifestation of such values.

From here on, the whole of liberal theology should be seen in the light of docetic christology. It understands Jesus as the support or embodiment of particular ideas, values and doctrines. Basically, it does not take the humanity of Jesus Christ seriously, even though it is in this theology that so much is said about man. It passes over his humanity, and discussion about Jesus gets mainly into the field of speculation and reconstruction. The understanding of the man as a bearer of a particular idea ignores his reality. It changes the real man into an ideal man and makes him into a symbol. This docetism has its most congenial expression in Hegel's *philosophia sacra* (sacred philosophy). Here the relationship of idea to phenomenon is brought to its fullest development. Now the phenomenon is no longer the accident, but indeed the necessary form of the idea. On the basis of a modalistic doctrine of the Trinity, Hegel sees the incarnation no longer as a semblance, but essentially and necessarily as manifestation of God in history. It is part of God's nature that he makes himself manifest. Only as one who is historical is God God. But this very 'necessity' of the incarnation is the danger. For that which cannot and may not be a principle is here made into a principle. God becomes man – that is *in principle* inconceivable. Otherwise we are not talking about real men, but about an idea of man. God's incarnation is no necessity which may be deduced from God himself. If perhaps idea and phenomenon may become related to one another by the principle of necessity, that would never apply to God and man, or God and history. In reality, this thesis also fails to do justice to man in his historicity. The incarnation is the inconceivable, the impossible, belonging to the freedom of God, the coming of God which is totally unpredictable.

Biedermann, an Hegelian, then proclaimed the dissolution of all christological dogmas. He said that the form of Jesus of Nazareth must be replaced. Christ must be the fulfilment and the representative of a principle, the principle of Sonship. Although Biedermann denied it, the humanity and the historicity of Christ had again become an accident of the divine substance. Docetism had entered the protestant camp in pure culture.

The Church must reject docetism in all its forms, because by it the being of Christ for the congregation is denied. With it, it will reject any form of Greek idealistic thought which uses the principle of antithesis between idea and phenomenon. Idealism takes away the first principle of all theologies, that God of his own free grace became really man. Christ did not realize a divine or even a human principle out of necessity. The nearness of every form of docetism to idealism or to rationalism makes it particularly fascinating.

2. *The Ebionite Heresy*

The Ebionite heresy does not spring from a pagan philosophy for which an incarnation is folly. For it, faith in the *cross* is far more of a stumbling block, an insult and a dishonouring of God. It tries to get round the fact that this folly of God is his wisdom. So it tries in its own way to make God's folly in the world wise. But here as well it is not possible for man to make it wiser than it is. God took the honour away from himself, so man cannot give it back to him.

Basically, the value of this way of thinking can only be appreciated in contrast with the pagan-idealistic way. It has its roots in Hebrew thought. The Ebionite heresy is the heresy of Jewish Christianity, which never gives up its heritage of a strong monotheistic faith in God. It tries to grasp the secret of the incarnation is such a way as to see the raising of a man to divine honours, but it is blasphemy for it to think of placing another beside God: the concept is *heis theos*, 'God', but not a 'second God'. Neither will it look to Jesus as an appearance of God on earth. Hebrew thought knows nothing of the metamorphosis of God so common to Greek docetic thought. The Creator cannot turn himself into his creature. Jesus remains a creature of God, a specific man. Jesus, the particular man, is the rejection of docetism by the Ebionite heresy, which thereby holds fast to the God of the Old Testament, who is no God of metamorphoses. It fails however to recognize the relationship of God to the man Jesus as an identity of being, but must stop at a qualified relationship. It therefore rejects a supernatural birth from the outset, even when it recognizes Jesus as *Kyrios* (Lord) and specially designates him as such. Consequently, as a second point, it disputes the pre-existence of Christ and totally rejects, thirdly, the deity of Jesus.

The baptism acquires a special significance. It is then that Jesus is accepted as the Son of God, who does the will of God. God's Spirit comes upon the mature, sinless man, Jesus. He is not God according to his substance, but receives a special kinship with God. There is a development in him. He *is* not God, but he *becomes* 'God', more and more as the Spirit takes stronger possession of him. This becomes clear to the Jewish Christian because he fulfils the Law, even to the point of being obedient unto death, the death of the cross. The designations of Jesus as Son of God alternate with those of him as a prophet of truth. Jesus Christ is a man raised to divine honours. That must not however be understood in the sense of the Greek heroes. In pagan-Greek thought the boundary between creator and creature is disregarded and lifted (docetism). In Hebrew thought, the separation is safeguarded (Ebionitism). The Greeks believed in the perfectibility of man, the Hebrews saw his limitations. In Jewish Christian thought, Jesus is a man, raised to Christ and Son; in Greek thought, Jesus is the man changed into a demi-god. They appear to be very similar in the concept of the divinized man, but their origins are totally different. Docetism and Ebionitism are often difficult to distinguish from each other, but they are fundamentally different. The one is concerned to remove all limitations from man, while the other is equally concerned to preserve those limitations. It is because the Ebionite stream often flows together with the docetic stream that it is so difficult to follow in the history of dogmatics.

The Ebionite heresy is represented among the 'monarchians'. They are concerned with the uniqueness of God. Their principal representative is *Paul of Samosata*. He diminishes the deity of Jesus and emphasizes his creatureliness. The deity of Christ is, for him, only the identity of will with the Father. The Holy Spirit is thought of as an impersonal power at work in Jesus. The baptism is the call of Jesus to Sonship with God. Jesus undergoes a development. It was because of this diminution of the deity of Christ that the early Church condemned the teaching of Paul of Samosata as heretical.

Liberal theologians have shown preference for Paul of Samosata and named him as one of their forerunners. True, there are some analogies, but this call on him for support is quite unjustified. Liberal theology is not Ebionitist, but of a docetic character. It is based upon the concept of the infinite value of man. Its statements point in the direction of the genius and the heroic. *A. Schlatter* comes nearer to Ebionitism. Ebionitism praises, not the man of infinite worth, but rather the obedient servant who is content to see God's honour as his honour. The salvation of man and of the Church is tied up with this servant. Despite superficial similarities, Ebionitism is superior to docetic liberalism, because it fixes its eyes upon the specific Jesus, the real man. Salvation will not be achieved through an ideal picture, but by the servant. At the same time as Ebionitism fixes its eyes upon the real man, it also sees clearly the creator God. What it does not succeed in doing – and this admittedly is decisive – is to find the way from the real creator God to the real man, the servant. Thereby the saving work of Christ is endangered and dissolved. Ebionitism cannot teach, at one and the same time, Jesus Christ as true man and true God. Therefore the Church must condemn it.

To sum up: the concept of the incarnation must be so defined negatively as to unmask every attempt to interpret either the fully human nature or the fully divine nature of Jesus, at the price of diminishing the one or the other. In christology, the humanity of God and the divinity of man must be held together, despite the danger of thereby threatening the rationality of the statement made. The concept of the incarnation must be so positively defined, that it finds a path between the docetic and Ebionite heresies. The question, 'How?', asked in different ways by docetism and Ebionitism, must be replaced by the question, 'Who?'

3. The Monophysite and Nestorian Heresies (Chalcedon, Lutheranism, Kenosis and Concealment)

1. Here the question of the deity of Jesus Christ will be raised. How can the person of God be thought of if he were to become really a man in Jesus Christ? In the development of the teaching of the God-manhood of Jesus Christ, the monophysite and Nestorian heresies arose.

The significance of the person of Jesus for salvation history requires that the historical salvation event should take place within human nature. For the monophysites, this human nature, i.e. our nature, must be assumed by God and thus divinized. The slogan was, physike henosis (Greek, 'union of the nature') – mia physis tou theou logon sesarkomene (Greek, 'one nature of the logos of God incarnated'). Christ is then not to be understood as an individual man, but rather as one who has put on human nature like a cloak. Certainly, he has suffered, thirsted, wept, but he did all this because he wished it, not because it was his nature. All depended upon establishing a unity of the divine and human nature of Christ. If God's nature were not revealed in our nature, then how should our nature be redeemed, saved and divinized?

This stands in direct opposition to the biblical fact. According to it, Jesus was an individual man with all the characteristics and limitations of a man, who wept, trembled and knew himself that he was not omniscient. Hence the Nestorians set out to preserve the biblical fact of the full manhood of Jesus Christ. Christ is teleios anthropos (Greek, 'complete man'). They thus saw themselves compelled to accept two separate natures in Christ, whereby the fully divine was kept separate from the human. The one, they said, could suffer, the other could not. A substantial union of both in Christ would be an affront to the Creator. One could only speak of a *schetike henosis* (Greek, 'attitude union'), an attitude of union of the will with God. The separateness of God was safeguarded, and the confusion or interchange was excluded. But what was overlooked was that while taking the humanity of Jesus seriously, the separation of the natures had been so stated that it was no longer possible to talk of an incarnation of *God*. In contrast to the monophysite emphasis, the Nestorians neglected the historical element of salvation. How could human nature be redeemed if one did not believe in a unity in Christ?

The controversy brought about an intense radicalization of both positions and made clear the insoluble dilemma of the doctrine of the two natures. The monophysites were dominated by a greater seriousness; the Nestorians, by a greater adherence to the Bible. On the one hand, the secret of a unity of human and divine natures; on the other, the necessity for a clear division. On the one hand, the mystery of the unity; on the other, the logical fact of duality. On the one hand, the divinization of man; on the other, the ethos in which the servant is raised, by conforming to the will of God. On the one hand, the question of salvation; on the other, the question of truth. On the one hand, passion, ardour, holding fast; on the other, the need for clarity. On the one hand, the priests, like Athanasius, although he was not yet expressly thought of as a monophysite; on the other, the laity, the ascetics, the theologians, of the type of Arius. It was inevitable that positions would become radical and controversy break out.

It came to a climax when the monophysite, Eutyches of Constantinople, declared: 'My God is not of like nature with me! He is not individual man, but only man by nature. He does not have *soma anthropou* [Greek, 'body of man'], but *anthropinon*' (Greek, 'characteristics of man'). This radical statement both defended *mia physis* (Greek, 'one nature') and also destroyed it. On the other side, the Nestorians over-stepped themselves when they replied by calling Mary *theotokos* (Greek, 'mother of God').

Thus the boundaries were laid down within which the early Church had to find its statements about the *Mysterium Christi*. On the one hand, it must reject the heresy of monophysitism, because there the human nature was ultimately absorbed by the divine nature, because it led to a speculation about the nature of God and man, and finally because of the statements it made about the identity of God and man. Monophysitism remained important for medieval philosophy. The early Church had, on the other hand, to reject Nestorianism, because in it the humanity and deity of Christ were torn apart, so that it was no longer possible to think of a unity of person in Jesus Christ, nor to talk seriously about an incarnation of God.

It was precisely against these two attitudes that the *Chalcedonian Definition* was directed in 451. This was the classical definition of the doctrine of the God-Man, Jesus Christ: *ana kai ton auton Christon – en duo physesin; asynchytos kai atreptos* (Greek, 'one and the same Christ – in two natures, without confusion and without change'). Those last two negatives are directed against the monophysites, because they make it impossible to think of God as a metamorphosis. But the Definition adds, *adiairetos kai achoristos* (Greek, 'without separation and without division'). Those two negatives are directed against the Nestorians.

The Definition was of the fully divine and the fully human nature of Christ, the *one* Jesus Christ with two natures.

What was actually said by this formula from Chalcedon? This, that any possible way of taking the divinity and humanity of Jesus Christ together as side by side, or mixed up, or related as definable entities, was ruled out *a priori* as neither possible nor permissible. What remains are simple negations. No positive form of thought remains to say what happened in the God-Man Jesus Christ. The mystery is left as a mystery and must be understood as such. The approach is reserved for faith only. All forms of thought are broken off. After the decision of Chalcedon, it is no longer permissible to speak objectively of the deity and humanity in Christ, nor to separate them from one another as entities. One cannot form a concept of God and then draw boundaries within it. The Chalcedonian Definition has been wrongly accused of forming the basis of scholastic theology, or at least being an expression of it. It has been wrongly described as the compromise solution of a theological squabble. Since the Chalcedonian Definition, anyone who attempts christology must do it within the boundaries drawn by the conceptual tensions of this negative formula and preserve it. The Swiss Constitution was right with its saying, *Dei providentia et hominum confusione* (Latin, 'By the providence of God and the confusion of men'). In its characteristic form the Definition cancels itself out. That means that it draws the boundaries of its own concepts by the way it uses them. It speaks about 'natures', but expresses the facts in such a way as to show that the concept of 'natures' is quite inappropriate for this use. It works with concepts whose formulations are declared to be heretical except when they are used in contradiction and paradox. It pushes the concept of substance, which lays the basis for the relationship between the natures, to such a point that it becomes meaningless. From now on, it will no longer be permissible to state anything about the substance of Jesus Christ. Speculation about the natures is at an end; the time has passed for any reasonable thought about the substance. If one is to think of any progress from the Chalcedonian Definition, it cannot be progress in thinking about the relationship between the natures, but rather in talking about something else which we shall discuss later. The Chalcedonian Definition is a factual, but also living, statement which bursts the bounds of all thought-forms. In its negative formulations, it is the ideal conciliar theological statement. It preserves with clarity and in paradox, the living statement of what from now on is going to be the orthodox doctrine: Christ is one person in two natures.

2. Within the protestant tradition, a great development has been attached to the Chalcedonian Definition. The formula, that Christ is one person in two natures, holds, but how is it to be interpreted? How can it bear the soteriological discussion and be true to the biblical material? And do that in Chalcedonian terms? The description of the natures must comprehend the fact that God is fully man. But how can Jesus of Nazareth be almighty and ever-present, and still be only a man? How could God suffer in Christ – and still be omniscient and omnipotent in him? The answer to these questions must be so given that it does not place the deity of Christ in question, nor make nonsense of his humanity.

It is with reference to this thought-pattern of two natures in one person that Lutheranism has developed the doctrine of the communication of properties in relation to the *unio hypostatica* (one structure of being). This is the most acute speculation that theology has brought to the christological question.

In this doctrine, Lutheranism holds fast to the presupposition that integrity of both natures in Christ must be preserved: the divine nature in its immutability and essential eternity, the human nature in its mutability and ultimate transitoriness. But before their integrated unity in one person, they had been thought of as isolated from one another. Thus one did what Chalcedon had forbidden. The human nature does not, for example, retain its human character on the teaching of the sinlessness of the human nature of Jesus.

The first statement then, after we have presupposed the isolation, goes like this: both natures are bound together in a *unitio* (Latin, 'combination') to become a *unio* (Latin, 'unity'). This unity is characterized throughout by the divine nature (mere active) determining the human nature (mere passive).

The divine is active and formative of person; it flows through the passive human nature as fire does through iron. The result is the *unio personalis* (Latin, 'unity of person'). From now on, this is the real and indissoluble union of both natures. God, *Logos*, is only there as in *sarx* (Greek, 'flesh'). He is only there as the incarnate, inseparably bound up with man.

This *unio* of *Logos* and *sarx* means the mutual *communio naturarum* (Latin, 'community of natures'), their full *perichoresis* (Greek, 'rotation', 'interchange') (John 1:14; Colossians 2:9; Hebrews 2:14). If the *unio personalis* expressed the unity of God and man, the *communio naturarum* expressed the uniting of the natures of deity and humanity.

The *communio naturarum* finds its expression in the doctrine of the *propositiones personales*. This doctrine declares that what may be said concretely about the particular characteristics of either of the two natures may be said concretely about the other. So that what may and must be said is that the man, Jesus, is God and also that God is man. But what cannot and may not be said is that deity is humanity, nor conversely, that humanity is deity. Thus the characteristics of God or of man may be predicated of each other, but the integrity of each nature is still safeguarded.

When the union of the two natures is thus described, it makes possible the most decisive part of this doctrine: the *communicatio idiomatum* (Colossians 2:9). This teaches the mutual participation and exchange of the individual properties of the natures. This is considered in three ways: a) The *genus idiomaticum*, the first *genus*. That means that whatever is true or is said of one or the other nature can be ascribed to the whole person of the God-Man. 'Jesus is born', can thus also be said as, 'Christ, the Son, God is born'; or, 'Jesus suffers', can also mean, 'Christ, God's Son, God suffers'. b) The *genus apostelesmaticum*, the third *genus*. The saving acts which are ascribed to the person of Jesus Christ can also be ascribed to the individual natures. 'Jesus Christ makes us pure from sin', can also read, 'The blood of Jesus makes us pure' (I John 1:7). Both natures share in every office of Christ. c) The *genus majestaticum*, the second *genus*. According to the two *genera* under a) and b), it is now possible to speak also of the relationship of both natures, one to another. Do the two natures of deity and humanity stand in direct relation to each other, and if so, how? The explanation of this *genus* is for Luther most decisive. *Genus majestaticum* says: those things which are predicated of the eternal deity may and must also be ascribed to the human nature. We must also therefore say that 'Jesus is all mighty, Jesus is present'. What we have here is the *est* of Eucharistic Doctrine. *Hoc est meum corpus* (Latin, 'this *is* my body'). The humanity of Christ must also be thought of as omnipresent.

The *genus majestaticum* is the heart of Lutheran christology. But at this point also comes the conflict with what the Bible states. There is also a danger of the return of monophysitism, because the humanity becomes deity and it comes very near to a transmuting of the divine nature into the human. Article VIII of the *Formula of Concord*, 'On the Person of Christ', reads, in paragraph 5:

And inasmuch as the divine and human natures are personally united, i.e. in one person, we believe, teach, and confess that this union is not such a conjunction or combination as that thereby neither nature had anything personally – that is on account of the personal union – common with the other, such as the combination that takes place when two boards are glued together, where neither confers anything on the other nor receives anything from the other. But, rather, here is the highest communion which God truly has with man assumed, and from the personal union and highest and ineffable communion, which thence follows, flows all of human which is said and believed of God, and all of divine which is said and believed of the man Christ.

And this union and communion of the natures the most ancient doctors of the Church have illustrated by the similitude of glowing iron and also of the union of body and soul in man.

The theologians of the Reformed Church protested against this Lutheran christology and raised three objections:
a) The person of Christ thus described is no longer the form of the Redeemer of whom the New Testament speaks. The latter is more direct.
b) This Lutheran way of thinking presupposes a change in God. God's nature can never be man's nature. Essences or natures remain divided, only the persons become one.
c) In the *genus majestaticum*, Lutheran christology is not basically speaking of the real humanity of Christ any more.

Instead, they put forward the following: certainly, the Logos has entered the flesh, but not in such a way that he no longer exists outside the flesh. The Logos continues in his trinitarian relationship and therefore also *extra carnem* (Latin, 'outside the flesh'). He does not enter into any necessary, indissoluble bond with the flesh. On the contrary, there is a development in the human nature, it becomes gradually and completely the instrument of God and is anointed by the Holy Spirit. There is no *genus majestaticum* and therefore no divinizing of human nature. At the beginning stands the sentence, *finitum incapax infiniti* (Latin, 'the finite *cannot contain* the infinite'). The natures are not bound up with each other except by way of the person. So in contrast to the doctrine of the *genus majestaticum* this means that what can be stated of one nature, can be stated of the person, certainly, but not of the other nature.

What then did these Reformed theologians make of the New Testament statements about Jesus that he had power to forgive sins and to raise from the dead? Here they introduced the concept of *alloiosis* (Greek, 'alteration'). 'This is my body' must be understood symbolically. Luther resisted the concept of *alloiosis* with anger, because it did not allow the Word to stand as Word. The Reformed theologians said that while the Logos was everywhere, as God-Man he was in one particular place.

Calvinistic theology laid great stress upon preserving clearly what God is and what man is; salvation depends upon retaining the true humanity of Jesus. The Lutherans accused the Reformed theologians of thinking of the relationship of the two natures like two pieces of wood glued together and, in this way, destroying the unity and placing redemption in jeopardy. If Christ were only God because he was anointed by the Holy Spirit, then in principle any man could become God. The finite can hold the infinite, not by itself, but it can by the aid of the infinite!

The criterion for a decision must be sought in the Scripture. The abstract duality of the natures and the abstract unity of the person are alike unbiblical. Of course, Luther can speak of the deity and of the humanity of Jesus, as though they were one nature. For him it is important to understand the humanity of Jesus as deity. The child in Bethlehem *is* the one 'whom the whole world can never contain' (from the hymn, *Vom Himmel hoch*). Out of this develops the doctrine of the *genus majestaticum*, which lets the human nature be permeated by the divine nature and maintains the attributes of the divine nature. Luther certainly runs the risk of not keeping the nature of Jesus separate from the nature of Christ.

3. The danger of ending up with a divinized man or a 'spirit-filled flesh' was recognized. Post-Lutheran orthodoxy attempted to meet this by adding to the doctrine of the *genus majestaticum* the doctrine of the two states of Christ. In this way they could preserve the unity of the historical Jesus, whom the Synoptists depicted, and the God-Man redeemer, Christ. Christ had passed through two states: the *status exinanitionis*

(the humiliation) and the *status exaltationis* (the exaltation). The subject of the *exinanitio* (humiliation) is not, according to Lutheran orthodoxy, the one who is becoming man, but the one who has become man. This means that the incarnation is not the act of the humiliating Logos himself. The incarnation remains eternal, even within the Trinity. The incarnation is more inclusive than the concept of humiliation. The incarnate one undergoes the humiliation of his own free choice. Humiliation is an attribute of the incarnate one, not of the Logos as such. For the Reformed theologians, on the contrary, the incarnation is already the humiliation. For them, the subject of the humiliation is the Logos *asarkos* (Greek, 'without the flesh'); while for the Lutherans, it is the Logos *ensarkos* (Greek, 'in the flesh').

But what is this humiliation? It means *not* exercising the divine properties and powers through the human nature for the duration of the earthly life of Jesus Christ. The question then arises as to how this 'not exercising' should be understood. There are two possibilities:

a) As a real renunciation, an actual emptying of the divine possibilities in the humiliation.

b) As a concealing, so that the divine powers are no longer seen during the humiliation of Jesus.

Thus the doctrine of the two states starts the conflict between the *Kenoticists* (from Giessen, centred on Chemnitz, e.g. Mentzer) and the *Crypticists* (from Tübingen, centred on Brenz, e.g. Hafenreffer). They question whether Christ partook of the universal sovereignty of God, while he was on earth.

The crypticists represent the theory of concealment, *krypsis chreseos* (Greek, 'hidden power'). They insist upon the identity of the God-Man, as he is from eternity, with the incarnate one, as he has taken upon himself the humiliation, and that this identity must be preserved. Their concern is with the unity of the person. If the exalted and the humiliated is not one and the same person, all is lost. The one who must suffer, so they say, is at the same time the one who must not suffer. The kenoticists objected to this, saying that if that is so, then Christ has not really suffered, he has not really died. It's all pretence and illusion. Unwittingly, cryptic christology finds itself in the company of docetism.

The kenoticists represent the theory of renunciation, *kenosis chreseos* (Greek, 'emptied of use'). They insist that Philippians 2 has to do with a real *kenosis*; that Christ has really died, after he has really suffered. Their concern is with the safeguarding of the human nature of Jesus Christ. True, one cannot speak of a *kenosis kteseos* (Greek, 'emptied of properties'), a renunciation of the divine properties, but only of a renunciation of their use. Christ has continually held back in the use of his divine powers. The kenoticists find themselves approaching the Reformed doctrine of the *Extra Calvinisticum*. They also endanger the reality of the renunciation and end with an unreal procedure. Their danger is the splitting of the person of Jesus Christ.

Crypticists and kenoticists compromised with a meaningless formula: Christ, as the humiliated one, has used his divine properties when he so wished and he has not used them when he so wished. The question of the *ktesis* (Greek, 'property'), the divine properties, which is the real theological question of substance, is passed over or pushed into the background. Here and there, when God wills, man sees something of the divine properties lit up. But this tying up with miracles leads to another concept of faith. Faith becomes bound up with what is seen of God instead of with the hiddenness of the cross. The whole christological problem is then shifted to another level. One may hold fast to the unity of the person of Christ, the God-Man; but he falls apart into two different states. One may hold fast to the identity of the God-Man; but he falls apart into two forms, a hidden and a visible. But Christ is *always* the one person in two natures.

4. The doctrine of kenosis was taken up anew in the nineteenth century. Thomasius and Gess revived it. They did so for the same motive that underlies the Lutheran doctrine of condescension, even though the starting point was different. As subject of the humiliation, they talk now, not of the incarnate God-Man, but press it back to the Logos himself. Their sequence of events is not, Logos – Man – Humiliation; but, Logos – Humiliation – Man. The Logos humbles himself to become man. The subject of the renunciation is the Logos *asarkos*, not the Logos *ensarkos*. This change means a simplification in the picture of Christ. The renunciation of the divine properties lies, for these modern kenoticists, in the beyond, i.e. in a metaphysical act of the Logos. Thereby the historical picture of Jesus Christ is set free from the inner act of violence caused by the suppression of his divine powers, which dominated the earlier kenoticists.

The question of the character of that renunciation still remains. Thomasius tried to handle this by a distinction between the immanent and relative properties of God. The immanent properties are those which belong to God's absolute nature; the relative are those which tell of his relation to the world. Examples of immanent properties are holiness, love, truth; of relative properties, omnipotence, omnipresence, omniscience. Now, Christ has received and bears the immanent properties of God, but not the relative. This then means that the man Jesus Christ is not omnipresent, omniscient and omnipotent, but that he does display the properties of God in truth, love and holiness.

Gess did not hold with this theory, but went further. He said that in Christ, God has renounced his whole nature: he ceases to be God in Christ in order that he may gradually find himself again as God in the developing self-consciousness of Jesus. Biedermann remarked that this was the final kenosis of the intellect; there is absolutely nothing more for one to envisage.

The attempts of the modern kenoticists have miscarried for two reasons:

a) The deity of Jesus Christ is not made comprehensible, but so qualified that it only becomes a part of man. But everything hangs upon the fact that God in his totality and sovereign majesty is this incarnate one who meets us in Jesus. One of the first theological statements must remain, that where God is, he is totally there.

b) The humanity of Jesus Christ is not made comprehensible. The humanity of Christ is only enlarged by some divine attributes, so that Christ finally acquires the form of a demigod who lives on earth.

Thus the doctrine of kenosis tried to reduce the claims of the divine nature until ultimately divine and human nature would fit together. A concept of God and a concept of man were worked out and so fitted together that they could not come apart. The smallest unevenness had catastrophic results. If the most difficult piece did not fit, the whole enterprise failed. In the event, the whole enterprise did fail.

A comparison with the Chalcedonian Definition shows that once again an attempt was being made to soften and balance opposites, which were both contradictory and exclusive. It had been thought that one could so define the divine and human nature *in abstracto* that they could be fitted into each other. But in that way, one only fell into the trap of oversimplifying the problems; the recognition of the real Jesus Christ was made into the recognition of a reconstruction of a God-Man. The prohibition against using objectifying categories for the solution of the question about the God-Man relationship had been disregarded.

Within the Lutheran doctrine of the *communicatio idiomatum* the doctrine of kenosis was a necessary supplement to the *genus majestaticum.*

But the kenoticists added alongside this the *genus tapeinoticum* (Greek, 'humility'). With the doctrine of kenosis, the

Lutheran dogmatic theologians were in danger of rejecting the 'two nature' teaching of the Chalcedonian Definition, in so far as at one place they overstepped its negative definition. A christological statement was constructed, i.e. the question, 'How?', was answered instead of the plain question, 'Who?' The Chalcedonian Definition had also given an answer to the question, 'How?'; but in its answer, the question, 'How?', was already superseded. It had, in fact, superseded the doctrine of the two natures by its firm adherence to the negative in contradictory opposites. In reality, it says that the matter of Jesus Christ is not to be settled with the concept of 'natures', neither is it possible to bring a demonstrable unity that way. This critical sense of the Chalcedonian Definition can take us further. This can only happen when the idea of deity and humanity as something which can be discovered is superseded, and discussion no longer starts from the isolated natures. The starting point is given: the man Jesus *is* the Christ, *is* God. This '*is*' may no longer be derived. It is the presupposition of all the thinking and must not be constructed as a conclusion. Since Chalcedon, it is no longer possible to ask how the natures can be thought of as different while the person remains one, but quite clearly *who* is this man, of whom it is declared, 'He is God'?

4. *The Subordinationist and Modalistic Heresies*

Here, within the statements of Sonship, we are concerned with the *homoousia* (Greek, 'same substance') of Jesus Christ with God. If it is not permissible to speak of *homoousia*, then once again everything is at stake. The concept of *homoousia* has undergone some changes. Here it is to be understood, not as likeness of being, but identity of being. Why is the statement of the identity of being of Christ with the Father necessary and firmly to be held? Only thus can the biblical witness that God reveals himself in Christ be sustained. Only then can we talk of a revelation of God. In the concept of revelation it is presupposed that God is identical with himself in his revelation. Otherwise we are not strictly concerned with a revelation, but with a manifestation or an idea.

The sentence, that God became man, compels the statement that Jesus Christ is identical in being with God. One tried to come up with the *homoiousia* (Greek, 'like substance'), but this formula takes us already along the road to Arius, who advocated the *anomoios* (Greek, 'unlikeness').

The *Subordinationists* based everything upon maintaining the unity and monarchy of God. If it were necessary to accept a second God, that was threatened and destroyed. Jesus must therefore be thought of as *anomoios* or at most *homoios* God ('different from or at most like God'). It was only thus that the unity of God could be preserved. But this was at the cost of the revelation. For there is revelation only when it is possible to speak of the identity of nature of the Son. And only in this kind of revelation can the decision about my life be perceived. So one is manoeuvred into the alternative: unity of God or revelation of God? Here lies the error of every subordinationist christology. It did not even succeed in preserving the unity of God. It is this 'either-or' which really threatens the unity of God. When Christ is understood as man raised to divine honours, who in his nature is not God but man, who is worshipped as a demigod, between God and man, then the unity of God is completely threatened. Then the door is opened to polytheism. Where man cuts short God's revelation for the sake of his unity, then this unity itself is destroyed. Modern Arianism, which honours Jesus as a genius or hero, threatens God's unity with his revelation.

Modalism was an enlightened attempt to hold together both the unity and the revelation of God. Christ is the *prosopon* (Greek, 'personal appearance') of God, i.e. the form in which he appears, the second of God's three forms (Schleiermacher). The modalists, however, need to be asked whether they really take the revelation seriously. Does God in his completeness meet with man? Is even his unity safeguarded? Or is it damaged by the fact that we are bound to an appearance rather than to the true God?

The concept of revelation and monotheism support each other. A qualified concept of revelation destroys monotheism. Either Christ, as revelation of God, is identical in being with God, or monotheism breaks down at the point of revelation. Subordinationists and modalists are at one in refusing to take the full revelation seriously and offering false solutions – the former with the adopted Son, the latter with the Christ-*prosopon*. The person of Christ is indissolubly linked with the inter-relation of full revelation and full identity of being. The formal christological principle of duality and unity is repeated: two natures and one person, two states and one God-Man, two divine persons (Father and Son) and yet, one God.

III. The Contribution of Critical Christology

Critical christology is concerned with differentiating and setting boundaries against a false Jesus Christ. Thereby boundaries must be drawn as much against false theological content as against unsuitable thought-forms.

Such sentences as make statements about Jesus Christ with unequivocal directness are designated as false in theological content. He who expresses the deity so unequivocally that it swallows up the humanity becomes a docetist. He who expresses the humanity in such a way that deity of Christ appears as the supreme human achievement, will be condemned as Ebionite. He who emphasizes the unity of the person of Christ, without at the same time expressing the duality of his deity and humanity, is rejected as monophysite or sinks into Nestorianism. Critical christology tests the adequacy of statements made in the light of what has been given about the fact of Jesus Christ. It prohibits any absolute statement to stand by itself and allows such statements to stand only when they are corrected by a contradictory opposite and thus checked. But, in this way, the thought-form has already been described, in which theological thought develops.

The thought of the early Church was sustained by the concept of *ousia*, nature, being. It laid the foundation of christological thought. Liberal theology thought that the introduction of this concept into christology had Hellenized and thereby corrupted the understanding of Jesus Christ in the Gospels. Opposed to this, one must say that in its own way there is no more 'un-Greek' product of thought than the Chalcedonian Definition. In the early Church, *ousia* is not to be thought of in the dialectic of nature and human culture (Ritschl). *Ousia* here really does mean the nature of God, the matter itself, the totality of God or the totality of man. The mistake lies somewhere else; not that the concept *ousia* turned the moral into a physical understanding, but that the nature of God and the nature of man were spoken of in a theoretical and objectifying way. In this way, the two natures were treated like two distinguishable entities, separated from each other until they came together in Jesus Christ. The relationship between God and man cannot be thought of as relationship between two objects, but only as between persons. In addition, nothing can be known either of God or man until God has become man in Jesus Christ. In this case, the advantage of the concept of *ousia* over a dynamic understanding (Paul of Samosata) is that this concept understands salvation as universal from the outset. From here on, the reality of salvation can be described in other ways than as though everything depended upon the dynamic act of will on the part of man, or as though the nature goes through a process of divinization. The liberal, dynamic interpretation also begins with two separate substances and does not remove the difficulty. It postulates and constructs the God-Man out of the previous knowledge of two isolated substances, instead of letting the presupposition come from the given facts of the God-Man.

This is the result of critical christology. The objectifying thought-forms, whether concerned with the natures or in their dynamic form, are ultimately rejected and put to one side. By giving attention to the facts themselves critical christology excludes these thought-forms. Only from the fact itself can one know who God is. The conclusions of critical christology can be summed up under three points:

a) In the Chalcedonian Definition, an unequivocal, positive, direct statement about Jesus Christ is superseded and split into two contradictory, opposing statements.

b) Objectifying thought overcomes itself immanently in coming up against its own limitations. It comes to an end where its contradictory opposite must be recognized at the same time as necessary with itself. The recognition of this end makes room for what is simply factual.

c) The question, 'How?', is superseded and destroys itself by its own formulation. It fails together with objectifying thought. Objectifying thought rules out the question, 'How?', because it cannot itself explain the union of God and man. When one has put the question, 'How?', to one side, one comes to the Chalcedonian Definition, in which the question, 'How?', has been eliminated. What remains is a pointer to the question, 'Who are you?' The Chalcedonian Definition is itself ultimately the question, 'Who?'

No christology can ever get behind these results and go back on them. How then can a positive christology be formed on the basis of critical christology?

IV. Positive Christology

1. *The Incarnate One*

The question may not run, 'How is the incarnate one thinkable?', but, 'Who is he?' He is not the one adopted by God, he is not the one clothed in human characteristics. He is God who became man, as we became man. He lacks nothing belonging to man. There is no gift of this world or of man that he has not received. This protest against *enhypostasis* must remain. Jesus Christ had his own human, individual *hypostasis* and his own human mode of existence. The man whom I am, Jesus has also been. Of him only is it valid to say that nothing human was alien to him. Of this man, we say: 'This is God for us.'

Two points of denial must be carefully made:

a) We do not mean that we knew something before about what and who God was, apart from Jesus Christ, and then applied it to Christ. No, this is a direct statement of identity; all that we are here able to say about God, we have gained by a glance at him, or better, this man compels us.

b) We do not mean that the statement, 'This man is God', adds anything to his humanity. That is the essential point. Against that it could be argued that something was added to this man Jesus, which we do not have, namely his deity. That is true, but we must be careful here. We are not to think of God and man in Christ being joined together by a concept of nature (being, *ousia*). Being God is not for Jesus an extension of his being man. It is also not a continuity of his being as man, which he goes on to achieve. Rather, it is a statement which comes upon this man from above. It takes nothing from him and it adds nothing to him, but it qualifies this whole man Jesus as God. It is the judgement and Word of God on this man. This qualification, this judgement and Word of God, which 'comes from above', must not however be thought of as something added. Rather than something added, this Word coming down from God is that man Jesus Christ himself. And therefore, because Jesus Christ *is* also God's judgement on himself, he points, at one and the same time, to both God and to himself.

Thereby what is avoided is the idea of two isolated given entities being united with each other. Jesus the man is believed in as God. And that, as man, not despite his humanity, nor over the top of it. In the man Jesus, faith is kindled in the Word.

Jesus Christ is not God in a divine nature, *ousia*, substance, being, nor is he God in a way that can be demonstrated or described, he is God in faith. There is no such thing as this divine being. If Jesus Christ is to be described as God, we may not speak of this divine being, nor of his omnipotence, nor his omniscience; but we must speak of this weak man among sinners, of his manger and his cross. If we are to deal with the deity of Jesus, we must speak of his weakness. In christology, one looks at the whole historical man Jesus and says of him, that he is God. One does not first look at a human nature and then beyond it to a divine nature, but one has to do with the one man Jesus Christ, who is wholly God.

The accounts of the birth and of the baptism of Jesus stand side by side. In the birth story, we are directed totally towards Jesus himself. In the story of the baptism, we are directed towards the Holy Spirit who comes from above. The reason why we find it difficult to take the two stories together is because of the doctrine of the two natures. The two stories are not teaching two natures. If we put this doctrine aside, we see that the one story concerns the being of the Word of God in Jesus, while the other concerns the coming of the Word of God upon Jesus. The child in the manger is wholly God: note Luther's christology in the Christmas hymns. The call at the baptism is confirmation of the first happening, there is no adoptionism in it. The manger directs our attention to the man, who is God; the baptism directs our attention, as we look at Jesus, to the God who calls.

If we speak of Jesus Christ as God, we may not say of him that he is the representative of an idea of God, which possesses the characteristics of omniscience and omnipotence (there is no such thing as this abstract divine nature!); rather, we must speak of his weakness, his manger, his cross. This man is no abstract God.

Strictly speaking we should not talk of the incarnation, but of the incarnate one. The former interest arises out of the

question, 'How?' The question, 'How?', for example, underlies the hypothesis of the virgin birth. Both historically and
dogmatically it can be questioned. The biblical witness is
ambiguous. If the biblical witness gave clear evidence of the
fact, then the dogmatic obscurity might not have been so
important. The doctrine of the virgin birth is meant to express
the incarnation of God, not only the fact of the incarnate one.
But does it not fail at the decisive point of the incarnation,
namely that in it Jesus has not become man just like us? The
question remains open, as and because it is already open in the
Bible.

The incarnate one is the glorified God: 'The Word was
made flesh and we beheld his glory'. God glorifies himself in
man. That is the ultimate secret of the Trinity. The humanity
is taken up into the Trinity. Not from all eternity, but 'from
now on even unto eternity'; the trinitarian God is seen as the
incarnate one. The glorification of God in the flesh is now at
the same time, the glorification of man, who shall have life
through eternity with the trinitarian God. This does not mean
that we should see the incarnation of God as God's judgement
on man. God remains the incarnate one even in the Last
Judgement. The incarnation is the message of the glorification
of God, who sees his honour in becoming man. It must be
noted that the incarnation is first and foremost true revelation,
of the Creator in the creature, and not veiled revelation. Jesus
Christ is the unveiled image of God.

The incarnation of God may not be thought of as derived
from an idea of God, in which something of humanity already
belongs to the idea of God – as in Hegel. Here we speak of the
biblical witness, 'We saw his glory'. If the incarnation is thus
spoken of as the glorification of God, it is not permissible to
slip in once again a speculative idea of God, which derives the
incarnation from the necessity of an idea of God. A speculative
basis for the doctrine of the incarnation in an idea of God would
change the free relationship between Creator and creature

into a logical necessity. The incarnation is contingent. God binds himself freely to the creature and freely glorifies himself in the incarnate one.

Why does that sound strange and improbable? Because the revelation of the incarnation in Jesus Christ is not visibly a glorification of God. Because this incarnate one is also the crucified.

2. *The Humiliated One and the Exalted One*

When we look at the humiliation and the exaltation, we do not ask about the divine and human natures, but about the modes of existence as man. We do not know a deity or a humanity in its own nature. We are concerned about the modes of existence of the one who has become man. Humiliation does not signify that the incarnate one is more man and less God, that there is thus a shrinking of the state of God – and exaltation does not signify that in it he is more God and less man. In humiliation and in exaltation, Jesus remains wholly man and wholly God. The statement, 'This is God', must be made in exactly the same way about the humiliated one as about the exalted one.

Of the humiliated one we say, 'This is God'. He makes none of the divine properties evident in his death. On the contrary, we see a man doubting God as he dies. But of this man we say, 'This is God'. He who cannot do that does not know what it means for God to become man. In the incarnation God reveals himself without concealment. In the way he exists as the humiliated one he is not the Logos, the deity, nor the humanity of Christ, but the whole person of the God-Man. He is veiled in the hiddenness of this stumbling block. The principle of the humiliation is not the humanity of Christ, but the *homoioma sarkos* (Romans 8:3, 'the likeness of sinful flesh'). With the exaltation this is done away, but the humanity of Christ remains eternally.

The question is no longer, '*How* can God be the humiliated man?', but rather, '*Who* is the humiliated God-Man?' The doctrine of the incarnation and the doctrine of the humiliation must be strictly distinguished from each other. The mode of existence of the humiliation is an act of the incarnate one. Of course, that does not mean that one can separate him temporally from the act of incarnation. Rather, the God-Man in history is always and already the humiliated God-Man from the manger to the cross.

In what way does this special mode of existence of the humiliation express itself? In this way, that Christ takes sinful flesh. The humiliation is necessitated by the world under the curse. The incarnation is related to the first creation; the humiliation is related to the fallen creation. In the humiliation, Christ, of his own free will, enters the world of sin and death. He enters it in such a way as to hide himself in it in weakness and not to be recognized as God-Man. He does not enter in kingly robes of a *morphe theou* (Greek, 'form of God'). His claim, which he as God-Man raises in this form, must provoke contradiction and hostility. He goes incognito, as a beggar among beggars, as an outcast among outcasts, as despairing among the despairing, as dying among the dying. He also goes as sinner among sinners, yet how truly as the *peccator pessimus* (Luther, Latin, 'the worst sinner'), as sinless among sinners. And here lies the central problem of christology.

The doctrine of the sinlessness of Jesus is not one *locus* (Latin, 'position') among others. It is a central point at which all that is said is decided. The question is: Has Jesus as the humiliated God-Man entered fully into human sin? Was he man with sin as we are? If not, has he then really become man? If not, can he then really help? And if he has, how can he help us out of our trouble, while he is set in the same trouble?

Here it is necessary to understand what the *homoioma sarkos* can mean. What is meant is the real image of human flesh. His *sarx* is our *sarx*. It is of the very nature of our *sarx* that we are tempted to sin and self-will. Christ has taken upon him all that flesh is heir to. But to what extent does he differ from us? First, not at all. He is man as we are, he is tempted in all points like as we are, yet much more dangerously than we are. Also in his flesh was the law which is contrary to God's will. He was not the perfect good. At all times he stood in conflict. He did things which, at least from outside, looked like sin. He became angry, he was harsh to his mother, he escaped from his enemies, he broke the Law of his people, he stirred up revolt against the rulers and religious men of his country. He must have appeared a sinner in the eyes of men. Beyond recognition, he stepped into man's sinful way of existence.

But all depends upon the fact that it was *he* who assumed the flesh with its tendency to sin and self-will. It was *he* who did the things that seemed to the onlooker to be sin and failure and must be evaluated as such. But because it is *he* who does this, these statements appear in a different light. It is really human flesh that he carries – but because *he* carries it, this flesh is robbed of its rights. He pronounces the judgement on his doings. He has anguish as we do, but it is *his* anguish; he is tempted as we are, but it is *his* temptation; he is condemned as we are, but because it is *he* who is condemned, we are saved through him. Because of this '*he*', the hardest and most scandalous statements must be risked against this humiliated God-Man and be borne. He is really made sin for us and as the *peccator pessimus* he is crucified. Luther says, 'He is himself thief, murderer, adulterer, as we are, because he bears our sins.' With that, Luther describes the basic foundation of all christological statements. And as such, the one who bears our sins, and none other, he is the sinless one, the holy, the eternal, the Lord, the Son of the Father.

Here we can have no balancing of the two statements of sinner and sinless, as though by this means we may keep away the humiliated one from the *homoioma sarkos*. He is wholly man and gives the law its due and is judged, and he robs sin of its power. He is wholly in the *homoioma sarkos* and condemned as we are, and he yet is without sin. The *homoioma sarkos* is also fastened upon him with its realm of sin, but it is fastened upon *him*, who yet is without sin. Without trying to balance, we have to say, it is *he*, not the *homoioma sarkos*, who is without sin – but he will not be separated from this *homoioma sarkos*. Christology cannot by-pass this paradox.

Simply stating the sinlessness of Jesus fails if it is based upon the observable acts of Jesus. His acts take place in the *homoioma sarkos*. They are not sinless, but ambiguous. One can and should see both good and failure in them. When a person wishes to be incognito, one wrongs him by saying, 'I have both seen you and seen through you' (Kierkegaard). We should not therefore deduce the sinlessness of Jesus out of his deeds. The assertion of the sinlessness of Jesus in his deeds is not an evident moral judgement, but an assertion of faith, that it is *he*, who performs these ambiguous actions, *he* it is who is in eternity without sin. Faith confesses that the one who is tempted is the victor, the one who struggles is perfected, the unrighteous one is righteous, the one who is rejected is the holy one. Even the sinlessness of Jesus is incognito: 'Blessed is he who is not offended in me' (Matthew 11:6).

The humiliated God-Man is the stumbling block for the Jews, i.e. for religious, upright men. The historical ambiguity is offensive to them. The way *he* acts is a way that is not the way of the upright and the righteous. The claim which this man makes that he is not only upright, but that he is the Son of God, is incomprehensible to the upright, because it breaks through every law. 'You have heard it said of old, but – .' The authority he assumes is incomprehensible, 'but I say unto you' (Matthew 5:21), and, 'Your sins are forgiven you' (Matthew 9:2). That is the core of the stumbling block. If Jesus had not been wholly man, but had taken a divine nature, one might well have accepted his claim. If he had done the signs which were asked of him for proof, they might well have believed in him. But when it came to signs and wonders, he went back into his incognito and refused to give any visible evidence for faith.

Thus he created the stumbling block. But now everything depended upon this. If he had answered the question put to him about his authority with an evident miracle, then it would not be true to say that he has become wholly man like us. Then at the decisive moment, for the question about Christ, an exception would be made. For this reason, the nearer the revelation, the thicker must be the disguise; the more penetrating the question of Christ becomes, the more impenetrable must be the incognito.

When that is said, the form of the stumbling block must be such that it makes possible faith in Christ. Expressed in another way, this means that the form of the humiliated one is the form of Christ *pro nobis* ('for us'). In this form he purposes and wills us to be in freedom. If Christ had proved himself by miracles, we would have believed in the visible *theophany* of deity, but that would not have been faith in Christ *pro me*. It would not have been inner conversion, but simply acknowledgement. Belief in miracles is no more than believing the evidence of one's eyes in visible Epiphany. When I acknowledge a miracle nothing happens to me. But faith is there when a man so surrenders himself to the humiliated God-Man that he bets his life on him, even when this seems against all sense. Faith is when the search for certainty out of visible evidence is given up. Then it is faith in God and not in the world. The only assurance which faith accepts is the Word itself, which comes to me through Christ.

Whoever seeks signs to establish his faith remains with himself. Nothing is changed. Whoever recognizes the Son through the stumbling block is a believer in the sense of the New Testament. He sees the Christ *pro nobis*, he is reconciled and become new. The stumbling block which the incognito presents and the ambiguous form of the Christ *pro nobis* pose at the same time the continuing challenge to faith. Yet, this challenge teaches us to pay attention to the Word (Isaiah 28: 19). And from the Word comes faith.

How then are we to understand the fact that Jesus does in fact do miracles? Are they not a breaking of the incognito? If the incognito falls but once, is the game not up? Should we go along with liberal theology and see the miracles as superstitions of the time? Or must we not at last go back to the doctrine of the two natures, recognize a *genus majestaticum*? The miracles do not break the incognito. The world of the ancient religions was full of miracle workers and saviours. In that, Jesus does not stand alone. The realm of miracle is not identical with the realm of God. The miracles may well rise above the everyday happenings, but they are only one step up within the created world. The concept associated with miracle is not that of God, but of magic. Magic remains within this world. When Jesus does miracles, he thus preserves his incognito within the magical picture of the world. It is not because of miracles that he is accepted as the Son of God in the New Testament. On the contrary, his power is declared to be demonic.

Only the believing community recognizes in the miracles of Jesus, the approach of the kingdom. It does not see in them only magic and false claims. But the incognito is not lifted for the unbeliever by these miracles. The unbeliever sees magic and an ambiguous world. The believer calls it, 'kingdom of God'. Our age no longer sees the world as a magical world, but it still tends to regard the miraculous as an unequivocal manifestation of the divine. When it happens, the miracle remains ambiguous, and it requires an explanation. It has its explanation both from the believer and from the unbeliever. The believer sees in it signs of what is to be done by God at the end of the world. He sees, bound to the incognito, something of the glory of God: 'We saw his glory' (John 1:14). But the unbeliever sees nothing.

The humiliated one is present for us as the risen and exalted one. That in the incognito we have to deal with the God-Man is known to us only through the resurrection and the exaltation.

The incognito has already been lifted for those of us who are believers. We have the child in the manger, as the eternally present; the guilt-laden, as the sinless. But the contrary must also be said. We have not avoided the stumbling block by the resurrection. We have seen the exalted one, only as the crucified; the sinless one, only as the guilt-laden; the risen one, only as the humiliated. If it were not so, the *pro nobis* would be destroyed and there would be no faith. Even the resurrection does not break through the incognito. Even the resurrection is ambiguous. It is only believed in where the stumbling block of Jesus has not been discarded. Only the disciples see the risen one. Only blind faith has sight here. As those who do not see, they believe and in such faith, they see: 'Blessed are those who have not seen and yet believe' (John 20:29).

Between humiliation and exaltation lies oppressively the stark historical fact of the empty tomb. What is the meaning of the news of the empty tomb, before the news of the resurrection? Is it the deciding fact of christology? Was it really empty? Is it the visible evidence, penetrating the incognito, of the Sonship of Jesus, open to everyone and therefore making faith superfluous? If it was not empty, is then Christ not risen and our faith futile? It looks as though our faith in the resurrection were bound up with the news of the empty tomb. Is our faith then ultimately only faith in the empty tomb?

This is and remains a final stumbling block, which the believer in Christ must learn to live with in one way or another. Empty or not empty, it remains a stumbling block. We cannot be sure of its historicity. The Bible itself shows this stumbling block, when it makes clear how hard it was to prove that the disciples had not stolen the body. Even here we cannot escape the realm of ambiguity. We cannot find a way round it. Even in the testimony of Scripture, Jesus enters in a form which is a stumbling block. Even as the risen one he does not lift his incognito. He will lift it only when he returns in glory. Then the incarnate one will no longer be the humiliated one. Then the decision over faith or unbelief is already taken. Then the humanity of God is really and now only the glorifying of God.

All that we know today only through the encounter with the humiliated one. It is with this humiliated one that the Church goes its own way of humiliation. It cannot strive after visible confirmation of its way while he renounces it with every step. But neither can it, as the humble Church, look upon itself with futile self-complacency, as though its very lowliness were visible proof that Christ is present in it. Humiliation is no proof, or at least one cannot call upon it as proof! There is here no law or principle which the Church has to follow, but simply a fact – put bluntly, it is God's way with the Church. As Paul says of himself that he can be exalted or lowly, so long as it happens for the sake of Christ, so the Church also can be exalted or lowly, so long as in both cases it is the way of Christ with it. This way is the enemy of pride, whether it is wrapped in the purple robe or the crown of martyrdom is set upon it. The Church gazes always only at the humiliated Christ, whether it itself is exalted or made low.

It is not good when the Church is anxious to praise itself too readily for its humble state. Equally, it is not good for it to boast of its power and its influence too soon. It is only good when the Church humbly confesses its sins, allows itself to be forgiven and confesses its Lord. Daily must it receive the will of God from Christ anew. It receives it because of the presence of the incarnate, the humiliated and the exalted one. Daily, this Christ becomes a stumbling block to its own hopes and wishes. Daily, it stumbles at the words afresh, 'You will all be offended because of me' (Matthew 26:31). And daily it holds anew to the promise, 'Blessed is he who is not offended in me' (Matthew 11:6).

PART THREE

THE ETERNAL CHRIST

*(There is no trace of any notes on the third part of this
lecture series. It is thought that it was never completed.)*

A FOOTNOTE BY EBERHARD BETHGE ON THE LECTURES AND LECTURE NOTES

The Lectures on Christology were constructed from lecture notes, because the original manuscript was not discovered. Those thanked for the use of their notes and their recollections are Hilde Enterlein (later Frau Schönherr), Herbert Jehle (USA), Hartmann Gadow, Gerhard Riemer, Wolf Dieter Zimmermann and Klaus Hunsche. Otto Dudzus checked the text with his notes, as did Dietrich Ritschl. Responsibility for the finished text remains with the compiler (i.e. Eberhard Bethge).

The lectures were given in 2-hour sessions in the summer of 1933, in Berlin. There were probably 18 sessions.

(Gesammelte Schriften, Vol. III, p. 552)

INDEX

1. BIBLICAL REFERENCES

2. NAMES

3. SUBJECTS

INDEX

Prayer, 27
Preaching, 51f., 57, 71
Presence, 43ff., 55ff.
Preservation, orders of, 10
Proletarian, 34f.
Pro me, 43ff., 110
Propositiones personales, 90
Prosopon, 99
Protestant teaching, 54, 81, theology, 54, tradition, 89
Psyche, 77f.
Psychiatrists, 13

Reconciliation, 65
Redeemer, the, 92
Redemption, 65, 76, 79
Reformation, 14, 52
Reformers, 13f., 19, 55, 92
Renaissance, 12
Renunciation, 94f.
Resurrection, 14, 44.f, 63, 73f., 112
Revelation, 32, 37, 51, 53, 56, 58f., 98ff., 105, 106, 110
Risen one, 33, 43, 44, 48, 60, 72, 73f., 111, 112

Sacrament, 18, 46, 48, 52ff., 59, 65
Salvation, 34, 84, 101
Sarx, 77f., 90
Scandalon, see Stumbling block
Schetike henosis, 86
Scholastics, 37
Scriptures, 73, 93, 112
Scylla, 33
Second coming, 58
Self-affirmation, 29, -negation, 29
Sermon on the Mount, 17
Servant, 84
Silence, 27ff.
Sin(s), 38, 53, 59, 62, 77, 91, 107, 108, 109, 112

Socialist, the, 34
Soteriology, 37ff., 89
Spirit, 49, 83, 84, 93
State, the, 63f.
Status: èxaltationis, 94, *exinanitionis*, 93f.
Study, historical, 71
Stumbling block, 46, 54, 59, 82, 109f., 112
Subordinationist heresy, 98ff.
Substance, 88ff.

Teleios anthropos, 85
Testament, New, 14, 33, 51, 70, 92, 110
Old, 82
Theologians, contemporary, 12, Reformed, 55, 92
Theology: critical, 74ff., liberal, 13, 14, 69, 76ff., 80, 84, 101, 111, Lutheran, 55, 57, 89, 92, positive, 75, Protestant, 54, 64, scholastic, 88
Thought: Greek, 76, 82, 83, Israelite, 82, Jewish, 76, 82
Tomb, empty, 112
Transcendence, 28, 30, 31, 33
Trinity, the, 81, 94, 105
Truth, 49, 51, 53, 76, 96

Ubiquity, doctrine of (Ubiquitarianism), 56ff.
Ubivoluntarianism, doctrine of, 56ff.
Unio, 89, *hypostatica*, 89, *personalis*, 90
Unitio, 89f.
Unity, 86, 99, 100

Virgin birth, 105

Water, 53
What?, 36, 44
Where?, 59, 60

INDEX